Bookstore Tourism

The Book Addict's Guide to Planning & Promoting Bookstore Road Trips for Bibliophiles & Other Bookshop Junkies

LARRY PORTZLINE

Bookshop Junkie Press
www.bookstoretourism.com

ISBN 0-9758934-0-8
First Edition

BOOK DESIGN:
Marks Graphic Design
dmarks@paonline.com

COVER GRAPHIC:
Lance Lekander
lance1@gci.net

Bookshop Junkie Press
P.O. Box 6067
Harrisburg, PA 17112
www.bookstoretourism.com
info@bookstoretourism.com

Printed in the United States of America

For Deb, Dustin & Maggie

ACKNOWLEDGEMENTS

Special thanks to the following people for their inspiration, encouragement, input and assistance in the creation of Bookstore Tourism as a concept and as a book:

Dr. Donald Koones, Director of Community Education at Harrisburg Area Community College, for insisting that I pursue the idea in the first place;

Toby Cox of Three Lives & Co., Bonnie Slotnick of Bonnie Slotnick Cookbooks, and Nancy Bass of the Strand Bookstore in New York City, for their hospitality, generosity and suggestions;

Mike Campbell, Pat Cusick, Danna Kiluk, Scott Portzline, Ted Reese, Deb Wagner and Jean Waverka for their friendship and unwavering support;

Deb Marks, for her terrific design and hard work;

Dustin and Maggie Portzline, for their love and patience;

And especially Deb Burg, for being my partner and guiding light every step of the way.

God works the night shift.

About Larry Portzline

Larry Portzline is a writer and part-time college instructor in Harrisburg, Pennsylvania. His professional writing experience includes journalism, corporate and nonprofit public relations, government communications and freelancing. He is an adjunct instructor of writing and literature courses. He holds a B.A. in English from Elizabethtown College and an M.A. in the Humanities from Penn State University.

CONTENTS

For more information about Bookstore Tourism, please visit **www.bookstoretourism.com**.

To submit ideas or suggestions for future editions of this or other Bookstore Tourism books, including city or regional guides, e-mail **info@bookstoretourism.com**. All submitted ideas become the property of Larry Portzline and Bookshop Junkie Press.

To sign up for occasional updates and news about Bookstore Tourism, please send a blank e-mail to **subscribe@bookstoretourism.com**. Your e-mail address will remain private.

FOREWORD

America's independent bookstores may be going the way of the corner grocer, the mom-and-pop hardware store, and the local five-and-dime.

All too frequently these days, the bookselling industry announces that another bookshop somewhere in the country is closing its doors for good. Usually it's a venerable old institution that's been doing business in the same spot for several decades, but often it's a once-promising new bookstore that for one reason or another couldn't make a go of it. The announcement is generally followed by an outcry from loyal customers and local citizens who want to save the store from oblivion, but typically their efforts fail.

The most obvious "culprits" behind the independents' struggle to stay afloat, of course, are the mega-bookstore chains and online booksellers that dominate the industry. That's not to say that Borders, Barnes & Noble and Amazon.com – each of which sell billions of dollars' worth of books each year – don't have a right to exist. They do. And so do all of the other retailers that have widened their shelves in recent years to stake their claim as "booksellers": mass merchants like Wal-Mart, Target and Kmart; price clubs like Costco and Sam's Club; plus drugstores, grocery chains, electronics boutiques, health food stores and even some gas stations. It's no wonder, then, that when J. K. Rowling's fifth Harry Potter book, "The Order of the Phoenix," sold a record-shattering 5 million copies on the day it was released in June 2003, roughly half were sold by non-bookstore retailers. (Sears recently announced that it, too, will start selling books at its new, much larger "Sears Grand" stores, crowding the playing field even more.)

It's easy to point the finger of blame, but the retail giants aren't the only reason small bookshops are struggling. There's also the economy, high rents, low readership, commercial overdevelopment – all of which have taken a considerable toll on the industry.

So what can the independents do to survive? How can they muddle through when, together, they make up only 16 percent of the bookselling market?

The short answer is, by focusing on the things that have always mattered most to their customers:
- a diverse selection of books personally chosen by the owner;
- individualized customer service;
- a knowledgeable staff;
- community involvement; and
- homegrown events and marketing efforts.

Arguably, these are the same essential qualities that the chain stores are usually accused of lacking.

Indie booksellers are also tapping into a number of trends that might have seemed radical just a few years ago – selling books online (many on Amazon, ironically), expanding into the fast-growing used-book trade, and offering electronic gift cards just like major retailers do. Other bookstores have resorted to fundraisers, auctions, and even stock offerings to pay down debt, expand, or just make the rent.

It should go without saying that one of the most crucial ingredients for keeping bookshops open and independent is community support. Bookstores thrive in towns that foster education and the arts, that treasure their history, that don't turn their noses up at things that are quirky or different. People who live in these communities crave intellectual stimulation, and they see their independent bookshops as being at the center of that need – a place to lose yourself in a good book (or is that *find* yourself?), to meet friends, to share ideas, to discuss current events. After all, independent bookstores aren't just stores, they're gathering places – a home away from home. Sure, they may not have as many books as a two-story corporate franchise, but they have something much more valuable: personality, individuality, and a passion for the written word rather than the bottom line.

Also, you never know what surprises await you in a small bookshop that you've just wandered into for the first time. Many booklovers have summed up the experience this way: When you walk into an independent bookstore, you don't always find what you're looking for, but you often find something you didn't even know you wanted. Repeat that line to a true booklover, and he or she will nod knowingly. They know what it's like to find treasures in the stacks – books they might not have discovered anywhere else.

Is your community the kind that supports independent bookshops? Mine, like many others, is in the process of finding out. Before the superstores moved into the Harrisburg, Pennsylvania area a couple of years ago, there weren't many bookshops to choose from, except at the malls and the handful of excellent independents that, unfortunately, seemed like well-kept secrets. In fact, one of the indies recently closed after 15 years in business – a sad day for a lot of people. We've been blessed with a couple of new stores, though, so it'll be up to local booklovers to support them, and to prevent them from being part of a dying breed.

What about your town? Which independent bookshops haven't you visited for awhile? Which ones have you never seen from the inside?

You might want to stop in soon.

Independent bookstores are as important to this nation's democratic conscience as they are to its system of commerce. And if they're going to stay put, they need our continuing patronage.

"Save indie bookstores" is becoming a common refrain around the country. If it's not in your town, it ought to be.

Larry Portzline
Harrisburg, Pennsylvania
August 2004

A SHORT HISTORY

I got the idea for Bookstore Tourism in 2003 when a colleague, Dr. Donald Koones, the director of Community Education at Harrisburg Area Community College, told me about the "restaurant adventures" he'd been leading to New York City. These culinary excursions sounded like fun, and I casually suggested to Don that a bookstore trip to Manhattan might also be enjoyable and a nice alternative for booklovers.

Once he climbed down off the ceiling, Don immediately strong-armed me into agreeing to lead such a trip for the school. I'd never led a tour group in my life and was hesitant at first, but then I realized that I would certainly go on a trip like that if it were offered, so why not?

Not long after, I contacted John Mutter, an editor at Publishers Weekly, who was researching unique marketing ideas for an article he was writing about independent bookstores. Having long desired to open a bookshop of my own, I was a regular reader of PW Daily for Booksellers, the e-newsletter John edited for the magazine. John asked to interview me about the road trip I was planning, and it was during this initial conversation that I first used the term Bookstore Tourism. My feeling, as I explained to John, was that if travel agents and motorcoach companies can load tourists onto a bus and take them to outlet malls, why not independent bookstores?

Granted, millions of readers already make a point of looking for interesting bookshops in whatever towns they happen to visit, but this was something new, according to John. I found it hard to believe – and still do, really – but as far as the folks at Publishers Weekly knew, no one had ever chartered a bus for the specific purpose of taking a large group to visit another city's bookstores.

The college's first "Greenwich Village Bookstore Adventure," scheduled for July 2003, sold out in no time. The reservations went so fast, in fact, that Don insisted I schedule two more trips for the fall to handle the overflow. Astoundingly, they sold out quickly, too, and people were scrambling to be put on a waiting list.

That's when I knew I was on to something.

If a small college in central Pennsylvania could sell out three bookstore trips in a matter of weeks, there had to be many more schools and organizations around the country that might want to do something similar.

Obviously, not everyone lives within a two- or three-hour drive of a city or town with a heavy concentration of indie bookstores, but I realized that there were ways to adapt the idea to fit a wide variety of interests, for groups of all types and communities of all sizes. And the novelty of the concept could only help independent booksellers, whose struggles I'd been reading about for years.

So, what started out as whim – an offhand suggestion for an engaging day-trip with fellow booklovers – became a grassroots campaign. I wanted other people to get involved. I launched a website, BookstoreTourism.com, started sending out news releases, talking to the media, and generally bothering anyone who would listen. In all, I led six sold-out bookstore trips for two Pennsylvania colleges – Harrisburg Area Community College and Susquehanna University – between July 2003 and June 2004. All but one of the trips were to the 20 or so awesome bookstores in and around Greenwich Village; the other, to the equally fantastic bookshops in the Georgetown and Dupont Circle neighborhoods in Washington, D.C.

During those first 12 months, media coverage of Bookstore Tourism was steady, with numerous articles appearing in national magazines; in trade publications for the publishing, bookselling and travel industries; in academic publications; in regional newspapers; and on a variety of websites. I received countless e-mails as a result, from booklovers, booksellers, educators, librarians, nonprofit organizations and travel professionals around the country who were thrilled by the idea and wanted to start something similar in their own communities.

Some have.

Some are apparently still waiting for momentum to kick in.

Meanwhile, I've been exploring partnerships with a variety of organizations that are keen to adapt Bookstore Tourism to fit their specific needs, including a few libraries, a couple of motorcoach companies, two major book festivals on the East Coast, a large university, a university press, a literary publication, and the booksellers in a small southern city who are itching to draw busloads of literary patrons into their community.

I've also continued to receive support and encouragement from the booksellers on our trips who would love for more people to take up the Bookstore Tourism cause. Several authors – some you know, some whose names are just now catching your eye – have also urged me onward.

From small beginnings, as they say.

It's a start.

And that's where this book comes in.

As encouraging as all of the initial reaction has been, the reality is that a lot of booklovers have never heard of Bookstore Tourism, or if they have, don't know what it's all about. I considered writing a book on the topic very early in the process, but I wasn't sure that the concept would ever go as far as it has. I didn't even know at the time what Bookstore Tourism was supposed to BE. Friends told me to incorporate. Legal-types suggested I trademark the name (I didn't). Booksellers insisted – in the most emphatic and colorful terms – that I simply had to give up my day-job writing for the Pennsylvania Senate to lead bookstore trips full-time. Still others said I needed to find a way to make money at it, since what the colleges paid me didn't even cover my book purchases on each of the trips.

One thing I knew, and that well-meaning acquaintances didn't understand, was that Bookstore Tourism wasn't going to be an *entity*. Bookstore Tourism is something people *do*. I've said from the beginning that the idea is free for anyone to use, and that all it takes is a little creativity, a little planning, and a gang of booklovers – whether 5 or 50 – who are up for an adventure. And the best way, the most obvious way, to share this concept with others is through the medium that brings us together in the first place.

My hope is that you'll find this book useful and informative, that it'll give you some good ideas, and that it'll encourage you to participate, either as an organizer of bookstore trips in your community, or as one of the lucky ones who get to go along for the ride.

I don't pretend to be an expert on the bookselling and publishing industries. I don't have an MBA, and I'm not a marketing guru. I wrote this book purely from the perspective of a booklover who sees a need. Call me a dilettante if you want, but like most booklovers, I don't just bring my wallet into a bookshop, I bring knowledge and experience and genuine interest.

This book is intended to be a rallying cry of sorts – a call for people who want to support independent bookstores to come together and do something. What I'm offering is an idea that anyone can adapt to fit their own purposes. In fact, I encourage you to *take ownership* of it.

My favorite part of the bookstore trips I've led is at the end of the day when everyone is piling off the bus, tired from walking and loaded down with bags full of new additions for their bookshelves, and they beam through their exhaustion and say, "Thank you SO much. We can't wait to do this again." All day long I've been running into them in bookstores and on the streets, and invariably they've stopped and excitedly shown me some new treasure they've found, or told me how much they loved this or that bookshop. And even now, hours later, their enthusiasm never wavers.

When booklovers respond that way, and when strangers practically jump out of their shoes to ask where they can sign up for the next trip, you know you're doing something right. Their excitement about Bookstore Tourism and their desire to see it succeed humbles me.

I hope it'll do the same for you.

What is Bookstore Tourism?

WHAT IS BOOKSTORE TOURISM?

Bookstore Tourism is an innovative grassroots effort to promote and support independent bookstores by marketing them as a tourist destination and creating a new travel niche for booklovers.

The primary goal of this groundbreaking project is to encourage booklovers around the country to organize day-trips and other kinds of literary outings to cities and towns with interesting, fun and unique bookstores that people in their own communities may not be able to visit regularly.

Between July 2003 and June 2004, I led six sold-out "bookstore adventures" to New York City and Washington, D.C. for two small colleges in central Pennsylvania. Since launching the idea, I've received countless inquiries and expressions of support from people in the bookselling, publishing and travel industries, from educators, colleges and libraries, from book festival and "One Book" organizers, and from booklovers everywhere who are eager to get involved.

I hope that after you read this book, you'll be ready to climb on board with Bookstore Tourism, too.

The Mission of Bookstore Tourism:

1. **Create a new travel niche for booklovers.**
2. **Keep independent bookstores open through grassroots support.**
3. **Promote reading and literacy.**

Why should booklovers support independent bookstores?

There are numerous reasons to visit and support independent bookstores, in your town and all across the country:

- They're engaging, quiet and intimate.
- They employ passionate, knowledgeable staff.
- They offer a diverse selection that isn't always mainstream.

- They provide personalized customer service.
- They're actively involved in the community.
- They support the local economy.
- They serve as a public gathering place.
- They attract writers, educators, artists and others who have a professional interest in books.
- They create an atmosphere for personal enrichment and learning.

Sadly, many independent bookstores are struggling and even closing their doors, not just because of stiff competition from the mega-chains, online giants and suburban "big box" merchants, but also because of dips in the economy, skyrocketing rents for retail space, and the downward spiral of the nation's readership.

Should the large, corporate booksellers be condemned for creating overwhelming competition in the industry?

Some say yes, some say no, others shrug their shoulders and ask what the point would be.

I don't want to politicize the idea of Bookstore Tourism – I only want to promote the enjoyment and success of independent bookstores and to give booklovers another tool to promote reading and literacy in their communities.

Why is it more important than ever to boost reading efforts in the United States?

The National Endowment for the Arts (NEA) released a report in July 2004 showing that for the first time in U.S. history, fewer than half of American adults read literature in their leisure time. According to the study, "Reading at Risk: A Survey of Literary Reading in America," the number of literary readers – those who read novels, short stories, poetry or plays – declined by 10 percent between 1982 and 2002. The report also showed that young adults had the biggest drop-off in readership, at 28 percent. Overall, the study noted, the nation lost 20 million potential readers in 20 years.

NEA Chairman Dana Gioia labeled the revelations "deeply alarming" and called for a "national conversation" on the issue. He warned that if Americans lose their capacity for "active and engaged literacy," we will become less informed and less able to think for ourselves. "These are not qualities that a free, innovative, or productive society can afford to lose," Gioia stressed.

Conducted by the U.S. Census Bureau on behalf of the NEA, the study pointed to America's heavy reliance on electronic media for news, information and entertainment as a primary reason for the downturn. Americans have more disposable income, the study said, but we're spending less of it on books and more on television, movies and the Internet. This "cultural crisis" came as no surprise, of course, to the bookselling and publishing industries, which have been watching the trend worsen for years.

The NEA called on the government, cultural organizations, educators and the media to take immediate action to reverse the problem. Public response to the agency's entreaty, primarily in news articles and op-eds in the weeks after the announcement, centered around the desperate need for solutions. Those who quickly joined the debate strongly suggested that new, innovative ways to promote reading and literacy were required nationwide; that reading should be a more social endeavor, emphasizing a "kinship" among booklovers; and that more of America's bookstores should create partnerships with schools, agencies and other organizations to encourage literacy.

Bookstore Tourism is no panacea, but it's certainly innovative enough and effective enough to help accomplish these goals. I hope you'll agree that the concept could easily be employed in most regions of the U.S. as one way to boost interest in reading and to put literature back into people's lives.

If those who are truly concerned about America's reading habits are seeking something new; if they want literary partnerships; if they crave the kinship of booklovers; and if they aspire to a cultural community, then Bookstore Tourism can help to make that happen.

This is a social endeavor all the way. But it has something more that'll get people hooked for good:

It's enormously fun.

Who should promote and participate in Bookstore Tourism?

Anyone who has an interest in books, education, travel or the arts:
- Booklovers and bookstore addicts
- Reading groups and book clubs
- Teachers
- Writers
- Artists
- Historians
- Public and private schools
- Colleges and universities
- Continuing education programs
- Libraries
- "One Book" reading programs
- Non-profits
- Civic organizations
- Senior citizen groups
- Churches
- Bus and motorcoach companies
- Travel agencies
- Tourism bureaus
- Convention and visitors' centers
- Independent business associations
- Chambers of commerce
- Economic development agencies
- Downtown revitalization projects
- State and local governments
- Book festival organizers
- The media
- And let's not forget booksellers and publishers!

The list goes on ...

So what's your particular field of interest, and where does it fit in?

It's important to realize that the idea can work in either direction: your group can organize a trip to another city's bookstores, or people in your community – such as your local booksellers, business association or economic development group – can find ways to attract readers to your town for a day of browsing, touring and other book-related activities.

Depending on your group's goals or needs, Bookstore Tourism has tremendous potential as an outreach, economic development, community relations or fundraising activity. Your participants will have loads of fun, and your organization can raise money, awareness or good will. All it takes is a little imagination and planning.

Think about it: If two small colleges in central Pennsylvania can sell out six bookstore trips in 12 months, then the idea could certainly take off where you live!

Why Bookstore Tourism is a winning proposition:

- It's educational and fun.
- It promotes reading and literacy.
- It brings together those who share a love of books and the written word.
- It provides outreach opportunities for many different kinds of groups, organizations and schools.
- It encourages economic development.
- It supports travel and tourism.
- Most important – it raises awareness about independent bookstores and helps them stay open!

The Economic Benefits of Bookstore Tourism: An Informal Case Study

In all, about 270 people participated in the six bookstore road trips I led between July 2003 and June 2004, for an average of about 45 people per trip.

Five of the six trips were to Greenwich Village in New York City, which has about 20 bookstores in a square-mile area. The sixth was to Georgetown and Dupont Circle in Washington, D.C., with more than a dozen bookshops scattered across the adjoining neighborhoods.

Two of the most important questions on my trip evaluation form for these six trips were "How many bookstores did you visit today?" and "How many books did you buy?"

The answers were encouraging: The average number of bookstores each person visited was 7.5. The average number of books each person bought was 4.5, bringing the total number of book purchases per trip to about 200. Some people visited only one or two stores; more ambitious types got to as many as 10. Likewise, a handful of people bought very few books, while some bought more than a dozen.

With an average cost of about $15 per book – a conservative estimate since our purchases tend to be new titles as opposed to used – the average amount each person spent was about $67. The group average for each trip was over $3,000.

In all, the total number of books our groups bought during the six trips in 2003 and 2004 was just over 1,200, at a cost of more than $18,000.

Now imagine multiplying all of that revenue by the number of bookstore trips that could be happening all across the country, in cities and towns large and small, with groups of all sizes.

Using our trips as a model:

- 1 bookstore trip = **200 books and $3,000 in sales**
- 25 bookstore trips = **5,000 books and $75,000 in sales**
- 50 bookstore trips = **10,000 books and $150,000 in sales**
- 100 bookstore trips = **20,000 books and $300,000 in sales**
- 500 bookstore trips = **100,000 books and $1.5 million in sales**
- *The sky's the limit for helping indie bookstores!*

These figures benefit booksellers, obviously, but there are other economic spin-offs and social gains to consider. Imagine all of the local merchants, organizations and others in your community who could benefit directly or indirectly from Bookstore Tourism:

- The organization sponsoring the trip
- The bus company providing the transportation
- The travel agent making the arrangements
- The literary and historic sites visited
- The restaurants and cafés where the group eats
- The other shops and stores the group patronizes
- The owners and employees of all these places
- The school, library, organization or agency that you partnered with

If Bookstore Tourism takes off the way it could – the way many people say it will – the economic benefits in the first few years alone could be enormous.

Could Bookstore Tourism turn into a national grassroots effort?

If enough people get behind it, there's no reason Bookstore Tourism can't turn out to be as successful and as popular as the countless reading groups and "One Book" programs that have sprouted up in recent years. All it takes is interested folks like you who are willing to get organized and put together a "bookstore road trip" or related event to get the idea off the ground in your community.

Wouldn't it be great to see busloads of booklovers pulling up in front of your favorite indie bookstores on a regular basis? Especially historic old bookshops, or newer stores that could use the help?

Independent bookstores are a home away from home – for grown-ups and kids alike – and they need to be cared for and cultivated.

What can you do to support the independent bookstores in your life?

Consider organizing a bookstore trip!

A Word to Bibliophiles & Bookshop Junkies...

You know who you are.

You can't stop buying books, right?

You have piles of them lying on your floor at home right now because you ran out of shelf space a long time ago.

Most of them you haven't even really opened up except to write your name in the front.

It's a compulsion.

It drives your significant other/kids/ friends/relatives/neighbors (circle all that apply) crazy.

We understand.

The good news is – you're not alone.

There are hundreds of thousands if not millions of people just like you.

Booklovers are absolutely rabid about bookstores, the way some people go crazy for antique shops, outlet stores or yard sales: they can't drive past without stopping!

Book addicts suffer from a similar malady, and so far there's no known cure ... except to give in to temptation and buy more books.

It might interest you to know that Bookstore Tourism is an enabler of the best kind. And if it's any comfort, here's what some people just like you have said about it:

HENRY BEMIS:
Patron Saint of Book Addicts?

In a classic episode of "The Twilight Zone" called "Time Enough at Last" (1959), Burgess Meredith plays Henry Bemis, a nearsighted little bank teller who is obsessed with books and oblivious to the world around him. His wife and boss badger him about his constant reading, and when he survives a nuclear war (by sneaking off to read in his bank's vault, of course), he's happy to be left alone forever on the steps of the public library with all of the books he could ever want. But in a moment of bitter irony that only the show's creator Rod Serling could write, Henry drops his glasses and steps on them, leaving him virtually blind. "That's not fair. That's not fair at all," he says. "There was time now. There was all the time I needed."

Fans of Bookstore Tourism Respond

"I am extremely intrigued with the entire Bookstore Tourism concept. I do not belong to any type of an organization, but with some research and more information, I hope to launch some sort of travel in my area." – **Austin, Texas booklover**

....

"Just a short note to tell you again how much I enjoyed the trip on Saturday. Sunday morning I arose with two blisters on one foot, stiff back & legs, but with a glorious feeling about the books I purchased – so many treasures, I would have liked to read them all in a day." – **Trip participant**

....

"The whole concept is brilliant." – **Australia bookseller**

....

"I have to get on this trend right now! I could organize Bookstore Tourism from Sacramento to San Francisco!" – **Blog entry from the Internet**

....

"I believe that you've hit a vein and that you should be the catalyst for similar ventures around the country." – **Massachusetts bookseller**

....

"What a cool idea you've come up with!" – **California bookseller**

....

"My bookshelves are jammed even tighter, my bank account is even lower, so I am very happy to have been introduced to all of these wonderful new-to-me bookshops. I look forward to trying new Bookstore Tourism adventures with you in the future." – **Trip participant**

....

"Congratulations on coming up with such a wonderful idea." – **Upstate New York publisher**

....

"I wanted to thank you for supporting independent booksellers. As a new bookstore owner, I realize how difficult it really is. I know that by supporting other independents, you are also helping me." – **Wisconsin bookseller**

"I think the idea is wonderful and very exciting." – **Pennsylvania librarian**

"It's a great idea and I hope you have planted a seed that will flourish." – **Manhattan museum bookstore manager**

"I think your program is marvelous. I am a booklover and I thoroughly enjoy browsing independent bookstores, especially those that sell used books. I am pleased your program is a success. Keep up the good work." – **Travel publication editor**

"I want to take a moment to let you know that my mother and I thoroughly enjoyed our trip to Greenwich Village's bookstores on Saturday! We were able to peruse the shelves of seven of the stores and at each one, the proprietors made us feel as if we were frequent customers, taking all the time needed to answer our questions and filling special requests." – **Trip participant**

"The concept of Bookstore Tourism is wonderful! As both a reader and an independent bookstore owner, I am thrilled to see you promoting this concept." – **Manhattan bookseller**

"Congratulations on all the wonderful publicity you're getting on your fabulous idea." – **Pennsylvania publisher**

"I think you're doing the independents a great favor. Let me know if I can help." – **North Carolina bookseller**

"Love the idea!" – **Maine bookseller**

"Congratulations on coming up with such a cool idea. I think what you're doing is really exciting." – **New York City literary journal publisher**

"I read about your tour in Publishers Weekly and wanted to applaud the whole idea. Brilliant!" – **Manhattan bookseller**

"I admire what you are doing." – **Pennsylvania bookseller**

"What a neat idea you came up with." – **Seattle librarian**

"Independent bookstores can use all the help they can get! Thanks!" – **Washington, D.C. education journal editor**

"It's a phenomenal concept and I have no doubt that this is but the beginning of something big." – **Trip participant**

"I just want to tell you what a great idea these tours are! I am first and foremost a book lover and I absolutely love visiting any bookstore I can find – anywhere I can find it." – **Manhattan bookstore chain employee**

"I have been meaning to write to you for ages to tell you how damn cool that Bookstore Tourism is! It's such a fantastic idea, and I'm glad you're getting attention for it." – **Mississippi author**

"I think it's brilliant and hope more people get inspired to organize tours to other bookstore meccas." – **Washington state bookseller**

All of the above quotes are from actual e-mails

A Bookselling Industry Primer

A BOOKSELLING INDUSTRY PRIMER

To understand the need for Bookstore Tourism and how it can help independent bookstores, it's important to have some basic knowledge of how the industry functions: who sells books, who the major players are, and where they stand in the competition between them.

Who Sells Books?

Corporate chains like Barnes & Noble and Borders dominate the industry with their big stores, sizeable discounts, CDs, DVDs and crowded cafés. Their aggressive growth and marketing efforts are often blamed – many would say justifiably – for running independent bookstores out of business. According to Ipsos BookTrends, which tracks sales figures for the industry, chain stores account for nearly 25 percent of the U.S. book market.

Book clubs are direct marketers who offer their members significant savings off the publisher's price. Members generally sign up for a promotional offer of several books for $1, for example, and commit to buying several more books at regular club prices within a couple of years (after which they can earn free books with additional purchases). Based in Garden City, New York, Bookspan has a virtual monopoly on the sector with 10 million members in 40 book clubs, including the Book-of-the-Month Club and the Literary Guild, as well as numerous specialty clubs. The market share for book clubs: about 20 percent.

Independent bookstores are privately owned and operated. Some indie bookshops are very small and specialized, like the living-room-sized (but quite famous) Bonnie Slotnick Cookbooks in New York City's Greenwich Village. Others are downright enormous, like the legendary five-floor Strand Bookstore just a few blocks away from Bonnie Slotnick's. There are many independent chains around the country, as well, such as Barbara's Bookstore, which has locations throughout the Chicago area and a few others on the East Coast. Together, indie bookstores have a market share of about 16 percent.

Internet booksellers offer their merchandise on the World Wide Web. The convenience and discounts they offer are extremely attractive to consumers. Amazon.com is by far the best-known "e-tailer," but others like

Overstock.com and used-book specialist Abebooks.com are quickly gaining in popularity. Meta-search websites, which allow a visitor to enter a book title or author and select the best price from multiple results, have also become trendy. Bookfinder.com and TheCheapestBook.com are examples of these comparison-shopping sites. The market share for internet booksellers: nearly 10 percent.

Price or warehouse clubs like Costco and Sam's Club charge an annual fee for membership and allow customers to buy large quantities of products at a significant discount. Their books – mostly bestsellers – are heavily discounted as well, usually because they're remainders (overruns or leftovers), but often because they're offered as loss-leader promotions (below-cost to attract customers). The market share for price clubs stands at around 7 percent.

Mass merchants and discount department stores like Wal-Mart, Target and Kmart (the top three discount chains in the country, respectively) have proven to be strong competitors in the book industry, selling significant numbers of bestselling hardcovers and paperbacks at attractive prices. Sears recently announced that it, too, will start carrying books at its new, much larger Sears Grand stores. The market share for "big box" stores: about 6 percent.

It's important to know, too, that **used bookstores** are becoming much more popular, partly because their prices are cheaper than anywhere else, and also because the Internet has allowed them to boost their customer base considerably. Bookstores and websites that previously sold only new books, including Amazon.com, are quickly adding secondhand books to their inventories, driving overall sales of used books – whether online or in-store – to about 14 percent of the market.

Other booksellers include mail-order catalog businesses and numerous types of specialty retailers, including drug, health food, hobby, home improvement, gift, grocery, multimedia, sporting goods and variety stores.

Who Are the Major Players?

The top three booksellers in the U.S. are:

#1 Barnes & Noble, Inc.

#2 Borders Group, Inc.

#3 Books-A-Million, Inc.

Barnes & Noble is the top bookseller by far, with close to $6 billion in annual sales. Headquartered in New York, it employs 43,000 people and operates 650 superstores under the names Barnes & Noble, Bookstar and Bookstop, and 200 mall stores under the names B. Dalton, Doubleday and Scribner's. It also owns the website BarnesandNoble.com. Barnes & Noble has closed many of its B. Dalton stores recently due to declining mall traffic and, ironically, competition from the superstores.

The number-two bookseller in the U.S. is **Borders**, with yearly sales of over $3.7 billion. Based in Ann Arbor, Michigan, it employs 32,000 people and operates more than 1,200 Borders and Waldenbooks stores around the world, including nearly 500 Borders superstores. Waldenbooks is America's largest mall-based book retailer, with over 700 stores in all 50 states. Borders partners with Amazon.com to sell books online at Borders.com and Waldenbooks.com. In the past few years, Borders has closed numerous under-performing Waldenbooks locations.

Books-A-Million is a regional bookseller with its corporate home in Birmingham, Alabama. With 4,800 employees and $460 million in annual sales, it's the third-largest bookseller in the U.S. It operates 200 stores in 18 southeastern states, plus 35 smaller-sized Bookland stores. Its website is Booksamillion.com.

Although it has a long-standing policy of not releasing its exact book sales figures, **Amazon.com** is one of the most powerful and influential booksellers in the U.S. Its media division, which includes books, movies, music and software, had $2.27 billion in sales in 2003, helping the company to its first annual profit. Based in Seattle, Washington, it employs 7,800 people. Amazon.com partners with Bibliofind.com to provide a search tool for millions of rare, used, and out-of-print books. Its Amazon Marketplace program allows independent booksellers to reach a wide audience for a small fee plus 15 percent commission per book.

Business data source: Hoover's Online [www.hoovers.com]

A Brief History of the "Bookstore Wars"

- **Wave #1:** Competition in the bookselling industry picked up momentum in the 1970s and '80s when retail chains like B. Dalton and Waldenbooks became standard in U.S. shopping malls. At the time, independent bookstores tended to be clustered in large cities and scattered in small towns rather than in the suburbs; so as suburbia sprouted around the country and malls were built to serve them, chain bookstores became an important part of the local and national retail mix.

- **Wave #2:** In the 1990s, as the mall model began to fall from favor and more shopping plazas and strip-malls were built, Borders and Barnes & Noble continued their expansion with bigger buildings, bigger inventories and bigger discounts, thus giving birth to the "superstore." Independent booksellers knew they had a fight on their hands, and worried where it would lead.

- **Wave #3:** Another upsurge in competition for indie bookstores arose in the late 1990s as Internet shopping grew in popularity and eventually became widespread. Now it was possible to browse for books online (in your pajamas if you wanted), order them securely with a credit card, and have them delivered to your doorstep, all at a reasonable price.

- **The Future:** Today there is more retail space devoted to selling books in the U.S. than ever before. And when you factor in the almost immeasurable quantity of titles now available in cyberspace, the future of the industry and the role that all of its players will have are a guessing game at best.

Praise & Criticism for the Mega-Chains

So why are Barnes & Noble and Borders so popular? Why do they continue to dominate the market?

Here are a dozen reasons that you probably already know:

1. They have numerous, convenient locations.
2. They have a wide selection of books.
3. They offer substantial discounts and coupons.
4. Their stores are large, well-lit and comfortable.
5. They have ample parking.

6. Their cafés are nice to hang out in.
7. They sell other quality merchandise.
8. Their in-store events attract the biggest authors.
9. They have a large selection of bargain books.
10. They have clean restrooms and changing stations.
11. They serve some communities that never had a bookstore before.
12. Their mass appeal helps to keep people interested in reading.

Conversely, why do independent booksellers and many booklovers find fault with the mega-chains?

Here are a dozen reasons for the flip-side:

1. Their size and wealth give them an unfair concentration of power.
2. They've created a business climate that relies on their whims.
3. Their small, anonymous, centralized buying staffs dictate what millions of people get to read.
4. Their buying strength earns them preferential treatment from publishers.
5. Their discounting ability gives them an unfair advantage.
6. They aggressively hype "popular" books whether they deserve it or not.
7. They ignore new literary voices and non-traditional viewpoints.
8. Their stores all look the same and have essentially the same books.
9. Most of their employees don't know enough about books.
10. The customer is just another sale.
11. Very little of their enormous revenues stay in the local community.
12. They've aggressively targeted neighborhoods with independent bookstores, causing them to close.

It would be misleading to suggest that any certain percentage of booklovers come down on one side of the issue or the other. The truth is, millions of booklovers shop at the chain stores AND indie bookshops... AND online... AND from the book clubs... AND at their local library's used book sale. These folks take a more moderate view of the whole debate. They say that every bookstore, no matter how small or large, helps all the other bookstores. They say that the more people are exposed to books, the more they want to read; and the more they want to read, the more they want to buy. These people are more inclined to say, it's not about the bookstore, it's about the books.

Let's face it – real book addicts don't discriminate all that much. If we see a book we really want, we're gonna get it.

In the end, the real power in the bookselling industry lies with us. We just have to learn how to use it.

Some Other Challenges for Booksellers

Whether you're Steve Riggio, the CEO of Barnes & Noble, Inc., or Sam Marcus, owner of the Bookworm Bookstore in the West Shore Farmer's Market in Lemoyne, Pennsylvania, there are other challenges for booksellers that no amount of parking spots or former U.S. president book-signings can help.

There's the decrease in readership that I already mentioned; there are also the vagaries of the economy, the uncertainties of war. Heck, there's even the weather: the long, harsh winter of 2002-03, for example, was brutal on booksellers like no other in recent memory.

There's also overdevelopment. Retail sprawl has reached the saturation point in some parts of the country, leading local governments and developers to wonder what they're going to do with all of the traffic congestion and once-thriving, now-empty, "big box" stores they created ("the high cost of low prices," as some have called it). For indie booksellers whose rents soared along with the neighborhood boom 10 years ago, the current slide in business often means moving to a cheaper, smaller space or closing their doors for good.

Also, it doesn't help that the publishing game is wild these days, with corporate takeovers and "merger mania" shifting the power on a fairly regular basis. In fact, most of the mainstream books now on store shelves are published by only a handful of conglomerates.

The sheer volume of new books is causing concern as well. More new books were published in 2003 than in any other year, according to R.R. Bowker, which compiles the "Books in Print" database and assigns ISBN numbers for books in the U.S. Bowker reported in May 2004 that 175,000 new titles were published in 2003, a "staggering" 19 percent increase over 2002. Plus, there were 10,877 new publishers in 2003, up 2.1 percent from 2002, bringing the total number of U.S. publishers to over 78,000. Analysts concluded that small and midsize publishers were primarily responsible for the jump in new books, since the quantity from the 12 largest U.S. publishers increased only 2.4 percent in 2003.

These figures belie the fact that the demand for adult hardcover and paperback books, which make up more than half of all consumer book sales, was flat in 2003 – an incongruity that led the New York Times to ask in a headline, "How many books are too many?" (July 18, 2004)

With that in mind, many publishers are now exploring non-traditional ways to get their products into customers' hands. Some have started using their websites to sell books directly to consumers, not bypassing bookstores altogether, but certainly taking another chunk out of the booksellers' market share. The phenomenal "Harry Potter" series, for example, can be purchased on Scholastic's website, and the popular "South Beach Diet" is available on the Rodale Press site. Penguin Group (USA) announced in early 2004 that it too would use its website to sell books.

And just as publishers have become booksellers, booksellers are becoming publishers, too. Barnes & Noble and Borders both publish their own line of inexpensive classic books, offering reprints of titles that are in the public domain (and therefore require no royalty payments). Barnes & Noble's goal is to expand its publishing efforts to reach 10 percent of its total volume within a few years.

Booksellers and publishers are also keeping a close eye on the "e-book" trade, although no one is sure if the book-on-computer fad will ever take off, and on print-on-demand publishing, which would allow booksellers to store thousands of books electronically and print them on the spot when customers request them.

When the fifth Harry Potter book, "Harry Potter and the Order of the Phoenix," was released on June 21, 2003, it sold 5 million copies the first day.

Of those 5 million copies, more than half were sold by non-bookstore retailers.

"Retail Strip Mining" from a Bookseller's Standpoint

Chuck Robinson, who, along with his wife Dee, owns Village Books in Bellingham, Washington, wrote about the effects of the nation's over-retailed landscape in a column for The Chuckanut Reader: A Magazine for the Northwest's Most Avid Readers (Summer 2004). He compared today's suburban strip malls to the strip mining employed by coal companies in his boyhood home of Whatcom County, Illinois – a practice that "destroyed acres and acres of productive farmland and left in its wake large areas of unusable land." Today, he says, "the shaft mines of old have been replaced by a modern form of strip mining."

He goes on:

"That strip mining takes the form of out-of-state, corporate retail companies building their big-box stores to extract, not coal, but dollars from the local economy. Of course we need (or, at least, want) many of the goods the big boxes sell. But, at what (hidden) cost? Are we willing to sacrifice local businesses that contribute more dollars to the local economy and fund nonprofit organizations at a much greater level than non-local, corporate companies? Are we willing to have empty big-boxes dotting the landscape when one national company decides to take market share away from another? Are we willing to give up the civic involvement that locals engage in? There are certainly hidden costs to the retail strip mining... And, we can make choices that avoid those costs and negative consequences."

Reprinted by permission of the author

Why Are So Many Indie Bookstores Closing?

So what's happening with independent bookstores? Why are they struggling, and why are so many disappearing?

Just about every week or two, the industry reports that another bookshop – often a well-known store that has existed in the same location for several decades – is closing its doors. In cities and towns all around the country, independent bookstores are slowly fading away. In fact, some large U.S. cities no longer have any independent bookstores at all.

There were about 13,500 bookstores in the country in 1994, according to the U.S. Census. Seven years later in 2001, there were approximately 11,500 bookstores – a 15 percent drop. This indicates a closure rate of nearly 300 bookstores per year, or about 6 bookstores each week.

Here's a very small sampling of bookstores that closed in 2004, along with some of their circumstances:

Ruminator Books, St. Paul, Minnesota

Ruminator Books owner David Unowsky tried some creative ways to keep his shop open when the weak economy and a nearby chain store cut into his business. In late 2003 he held an online "Author Artifact Auction" featuring literary memorabilia donated by celebrity authors, including an autographed t-shirt from Margaret Atwood, a drawing by Oliver Sacks, and Paul Auster's broken reading glasses. He also tried selling stock in the company for $1 per share (at a 250-share minimum), but failed to raise enough cash. After 34 years in business, Ruminator Books – a St. Paul landmark and "literary oasis," according to its regulars – closed in 2004.

Midnight Special Bookstore, Santa Monica, California

The Midnight Special Bookstore, arguably one of the most famous counter-culture bookshops in the country, also went out of business in 2004 after 34 years. When rents in Santa Monica's trendy Third Street Promenade skyrocketed, owner Margie Ghiz was forced to close the shop to look for a new location. Finances and bureaucratic delays prevented Ghiz from reopening just a few blocks away until nine months later. By then she had to take drastic action to make ends meet, so she asked the people on her e-mail list to donate $20 each to help pay down her debt. A few weeks later, three independent presses sponsored a benefit for the store featuring a number of authors and performers, including "Lord of the Rings" star and published poet Viggo Mortensen. In May 2004, however, Ghiz announced in an e-mail to her customers that she would close Midnight Special for good, "with so much sadness and even much anger."

Windsor Park Books, Mechanicsburg, Pennsylvania

When Windsor Park Books owners Nick Marshall and John Kelley announced their closing in a letter to their regular customers in 2004, they cited a four-year decline in business that had begun when two chain stores opened just a few miles from their location outside Harrisburg, Pennsylvania. They said they'd worried that the competition might have "squashed" them immediately, but that it turned out to be a more gradual process. They said, "While the drops haven't been dramatic from year to year, the cumulative effect has been substantial." They also blamed annual rent increases for their decision to close after 15 years.

Avenue Victor Hugo Bookshop, Boston, Massachusetts

Author John Usher was moved to write a powerful polemic on the state of independent bookselling upon the closing of the Avenue Victor Hugo Bookshop in 2004. The piece, called "The Crepuscule: Twelve Reasons for the Death of Small and Independent Booksellers," was posted on the shop's website and circulated widely in the bookselling industry. In it, Usher blamed publishers, for "marketing their product like so much soap or breakfast cereal"; corporate law, "for making 'competition' a joke"; reviewers, for "promoting what is being advertised"; and the public, who "do not read books, or cannot find the time." He also chided booksellers who "push what is 'hot' instead of developing the long term interest of the reader." The bookstore, a Back Bay institution for 29 years, now exists as an online bookseller only.

Chinook Bookshop, Colorado Springs, Colorado

Dubbed the "best bookshop in the USA" by Town and Country magazine in 1975, the Chinook Bookshop closed on June 15, 2004, the 45th anniversary of its opening. Owners Dick and Judy Noyes, who opened the shop when they were in their 20s, pointed to competition from three nearby chain stores as a prime reason for their decision to retire. Regulars lamented the closing of this downtown landmark, which they said reflected the Noyes' personalities.

Hannslick & Wegner International Bookstore, Westport, Connecticut

The Hannslick & Wegner International Bookstore was renowned for its travel and foreign language books, as well as its rare and antiquarian titles. But after 17 years, owners Johanna and John Straczek could no longer compete against a nearby chain store that's been blamed for putting five other local indies out of business. The specialty bookstore will remain online, but for people in Westport – which now has only one independent bookseller – the loss of yet another was a shock.

John McCutcheon is considered by many to be the finest contemporary folksinger in the U.S.

When a favorite bookstore in his hometown of Charlottesville, Virginia closed its doors, he wrote this song about it.

"Closing the Bookstore Down"
Words & Music by John McCutcheon

I remember the night and the old wood floor
Dust on the shelves and a bell on the door
We were shoulder to shoulder, you couldn't fit more
We held our breath as one
Her voice rang out in righteous rage
As her poetry leapt off the page
Like a herald from another age
But now those days are done

We're taking a giant step into the future
And turning into a thousand other towns
I heard today the news that they are
Closing the bookstore down

It's a smile and a wave and a "take your time!"
We got just one way, we got just one line
And the till can't ring past 9.99
The time and the telling shows

We might not have everything that you want
You can't get a latte or croissant
We're a bookstore, not a restaurant
And we've got enough of them, God knows

We're taking a giant step into the future
And turning into a thousand other towns
I heard today the news that they are
Closing the bookstore down

Some big concern comes in and yanks
Our jobs, our shops, our hometown banks
Then they expect our grateful thanks
It happens everyday
I guess I just prefer to see
Success serve our community
Not some wealthy VIP
Who lives a thousand miles away

So, take a minute and look around
There are corner shops in every town
Squeezed and pushed and hunkered down
And battered by the blows
No, they might not be shiny or bright or new
But they're run by folks like me and you
Now, I can't tell you want to do
But me ... I'm gonna shop in those

So give me slow food and a hometown team
Spencer's, Bodo's, Chap's Ice Cream
Gleason Hardware and that corner store
With dust on the shelves and a bell on the door
I swear I'd love to hear that sound once more
Since they closed the bookstore down

©1998 John McCutcheon/Appalsongs (ASCAP)
From "Storied Ground" (Rounder 0467)
Available from www.folkmusic.com
Reprinted by permission

Success Stories

The news for independent booksellers isn't all bad, of course. New stores continue to open, and older stores continue to thrive despite serious competition. Some have even celebrated major anniversaries, which is a testament to their staying power.

Here are a few examples from around the country. They might even give you some ideas for a bookstore road trip!

Mitchell Books, Ft. Wayne, Indiana

Peter Bobeck wanted Mitchell Books in Ft. Wayne, Indiana to stand out from his chain store competitors as a community center and gathering place. And when his supersized general-interest bookshop opened in July 2004, his customers went so far as to call it a "village." Along with an extensive selection of books, children's literature, CDs and DVDs, Mitchell Books has a 65-seat screening room, a theater space, a cooking demonstration area, and a full-service bistro called Spoons.

Events at the store include author appearances, independent and foreign films, and dinner theater. Bobeck also did something unusual for his extra large children's section: he invited an existing kids' bookstore down the road, Mr. McGregor's Garden, to set up shop in his, renaming it Sherwood Forest.

Housing Works Used Book Café, New York City

In 2002, the New York Times called Housing Works Used Book Café "one of the hottest literary hubs" in Manhattan. Located on a narrow street in Soho, the bookstore is operated by Housing Works, Inc., a nonprofit organization providing housing, health care and other services to homeless people with HIV and AIDS. The store's enormous inventory is made up almost entirely of used and bargain books donated by customers, and by publishers who drop off boxes of recent popular titles.

The building itself is striking and spacious, with 20-foot ceilings, spiral staircases, a wraparound second-floor gallery, comfortable seats and a homey café offering light food and beverages. The friendly, full-time staff is complemented by volunteers, among whom are rumored to be some well-known writers (you never know who you might find behind the cash register). The store's events include readings by established as well as rising authors, and benefit performances by singers like Ryan Adams and Roseanne Cash. Housing Works' literary reputation is outmatched only by its "unusual mission," as one author called it.

[www.housingworks.org/usedbookcafe]

Changing Hands Bookstore, Tempe, Arizona

When Cindy Dach, manager of Changing Hands Bookstore in Tempe, Arizona, decided in 2003 that she wanted to hold an event for first-time authors, she knew it could be a tough sell since first books don't normally draw big crowds. Figuring that five new authors might bring in five times the people, she organized "First Fiction 2003" and held it at on the patio of a local restaurant near Arizona State University. Free food and five-cent first drinks helped to attract an audience to the event, which featured the authors reading from their work, Q&A, book-signing and plenty of mingling. "It was a huge success," says Dach. "We had about 100 people and everyone stayed all night. We even had people stopping on the street to listen."

In 2004, Dach decided to expand the event – nicknamed "Bookapalooza" – into a six-city tour over six days, with stops in Los Angeles, Portland, Denver, Albuquerque, Austin and back home in Tempe. "First Fiction 2004" featured five new book authors, including a Pulitzer Prize-winning journalist. The tour was sponsored by local bookstores and held at bars and restaurants in each of the cities. Dach is also planning an event she's calling "Whine With Me," which will feature three memoir authors and a wine company sponsor.

[www.changinghands.com]

The Reading Room at Mandalay Place, Las Vegas

The Reading Room at Mandalay Place is the first general-interest independent bookstore in Las Vegas. Located in an upscale mall on a sky bridge between the Mandalay Bay and Luxor Hotels, the shop is the brainchild of Mandalay Bay president and CFO Glenn Schaeffer.

Schaeffer said when the store opened in November 2003 that he believed it would provide readers with a refuge from the city's noisy casinos. With its dark wood floors, extensive selection of limited editions, and connection to the Chocolate Swan confectionery next door (which doubles as the bookstore's coffee shop), the Reading Room has been dubbed "a literary oasis in the desert."

[www.mandalaybay.com]

What are Independent Bookstores Doing to Survive & Thrive?

So how are independent bookstores fighting the competition? What are they doing not only to get by, but to make themselves stand out from the pack?

As I mentioned in the Foreword, they're focusing on the things that have always mattered most to their customers and doing them better than ever: a diverse selection of books personally chosen by the owner; individualized customer service; a knowledgeable staff; community involvement; and homegrown events and marketing efforts.

Many are also redefining their mission to become more like community centers. Indie bookstores are helping to fill the void that's been left as public gathering places disappear from many cities and towns. They're creating a setting where people can go to hear an author speak, to hear a local musician, to attend a seminar, or just to hang out with a book and a cup of coffee. They're also hosting reading groups, sponsoring giveaways, and partnering with other businesses and organizations to support local charities as well as each other.

Following are some of the innovative and even radical ways that many independent bookstores are setting themselves apart.

CUSTOMER SERVICE

Ask any successful bookstore owner, and she'll tell you that customer service is everything. Customers expect their indie booksellers to be experts in their field. It's not enough for the owner to be an avid reader, she has to know what's happening in the industry – what books are coming out, what's selling, what authors are hot, what kind of reviews a book is getting, which genres have finally exhausted themselves, etc. If customers can trust their booksellers to give them the inside scoop, they're likely to keep coming back.

Which brings up another good point: Booksellers should not only know their regulars by name, they should know what kind of books they like and who their favorite authors are. Customers appreciate knowing that they're more than just another credit card to swipe. "Handselling" – matching a book with a customer based on equal parts familiarity and instinct – is an art form. It takes someone who knows books, knows the market, and knows her customers.

Customers also love extras. They like it when special orders arrive quickly; when they can get a book gift-wrapped; when they can ship a book to someone they love in another state.

Unparalleled customer service equals customer loyalty – even when the chain store down the street might have the same book for a couple bucks less.

Used Books

One of the hottest trends in bookselling today is the used-book business. Many stores that previously sold only new books are exploring this niche as consumer demand for secondhand books goes through the roof.

Why have used books become so big?
1. They're much cheaper than new books, obviously.
2. There's something intriguing about owning a book with a history.
3. It's fun to browse secondhand shops and discover old books you've never heard of.

Ipsos-BookTrends, which tracks sales data for the bookselling industry, reported in April 2004 that used books accounted for 14 percent of all general trade book sales in 2003, up from 13 percent in 2002. In fact, used books have become so popular, Ipsos said, they're actually cutting into new book sales. Internet retailers have helped to fuel this trend by selling loads of used books at deeply-reduced prices, often right next to new, more expensive copies of the same title.

For consumers, the question comes down to this: Why pay $26 for a new book if you can buy it *almost* new for half that much?

Booksellers like to sell used books because their profit margins are higher. For example, if a bookseller buys a used book for $2 and sells it for $10, that's a gross profit of $8, or four times the amount she paid for it. This is much more lucrative than a new book, which might cost the bookseller $11.70 wholesale, sell for $26 retail, and generate a gross profit of $14.30, or 22 percent more than what she paid.

There are many other factors that go into a bookseller's choice of selling new or used books, but dollar-for-dollar, used books generate more profit.

EVENTS & ENTERTAINMENT

One of the best promotional tools for indie booksellers is special events. Some bookstores can hold a dozen events or more a month, while others are happy with just one. To use an extreme example, **Politics & Prose** in Washington, D.C. has author events almost every night of the week, plus loads of children's programs and workshops.

The most successful indies are always looking for some new, tantalizing get-together to excite the community, like wine-tastings by candlelight, over-50 singles mixers, island-themed travel seminars, holiday feasts, and crafts fairs for kids, just to name a few.

When **Northern Lights Books & Gifts** in Duluth, Minnesota celebrated its 10th anniversary in 2003, it didn't just hold a 10 percent off sale or hand out cake to its customers, it put on three major events in six months, including a gala reception to celebrate the works of regional authors. "One-third of the store has a regional emphasis," says owner Anita Zager. "Without our local authors, we wouldn't be in business."

With that in mind, Northern Lights held an evening of readings and music called "Light Up the Night" at the former Duluth train station, which now serves as a railroad museum. The celebration helped to raise money for the depot and featured regional poets, a short story writer and local musicians, all of whose works were offered for sale. Close to 100 people attended, Zager says. "We wanted to thank the community and our regional authors, and we wanted to let people know that we're here and we're going strong," she notes.

The store also held a "Harry Potter" book release party at the station, complete with a "Hogwarts Express" train that pulled in at midnight. A visit by well-known children's author Jan Brett ("On Noah's Ark") rounded out the anniversary series, with 500 people in attendance.

[Politics & Prose: www.politics-prose.com]
[Northern Lights Books & Gifts: www.norlights.com]

BOOKSTORE TOURISM TIP:

Before your bookstore road trip, check with the booksellers on your list to see what events they might have planned for that day, especially author visits. Some bookstores may even be willing to coordinate something special just for you!

Atmosphere & Décor

Many independent bookstores have undergone makeovers to achieve the perfect balance between functionality and fun. Their owners understand that a bookstore visit should be a comfortable, aesthetically pleasing experience, and that the judgment call a customer makes when she walks through the door affects their bottom line.

In 2000, the **Valley Bookseller** in Stillwater, Minnesota moved out of its strip mall location into a waterfront property along the beautiful and historic St. Croix River. Co-owner Joci Tilsen says she and her partners wanted to create a store that reflects the natural, outdoor quality of the community, so they chose a design that incorporates nautical and wildlife elements, including an aviary with exotic birds. "Children love to come in and see if there are any new additions," Tilsen says. "The birds lay eggs every few weeks, and people like watching the adult birds teach their babies to fly."

The store also has a reading lounge with large windows to let in the natural light, a children's loft with a long curved bench and bean bag chairs in a storytime area, and a large event space for author readings, book club meetings and other community gatherings. Out back there's a deck with tables and chairs overlooking the river – a popular spot for readers during the warm weather months, Tilsen notes. "A lot of first-time visitors say the store is very unexpected," she says. "They say it's very comfortable and fits in well with the community."

Tilsen predicts that it's only a matter of time until "one of the 'big box' stores" moves into Stillwater. "We wanted to be proactive and create a large store with enough amenities that will provide a pleasant experience for our customers and encourage their loyalty," she says.

[www.valleybookseller.com]

BOOKSTORE TOURISM TIP:

Many of the best indie bookshops are small and strictly utilitarian, with bare-bones furnishings, old art posters on the wall and stacks of books on the floor. Most booklovers aren't so finicky that they won't go into a place like this, because they know that's where they're liable to find the one book they couldn't track down anywhere else! This rule usually applies: *Funky means fun.*

CAFÉS & ALCOHOL

Cafés are nearly ubiquitous in the largest bookstores, but even the smallest bookshops that have them generally find that they help their bottom line because they sell more products and encourage customers to linger.

Some bookstores, like **Kramerbooks & Afterwords** in Washington, D.C., are known as much for their cafés as they are for their books. Kramerbooks has taken the café model to the extreme, in fact, creating an extraordinarily popular, full-service bistro in the back of its store in Dupont Circle. There's also an enormous pastry case with fresh goodies, and for those who like their coffee Irish, a full bar, complete with Internet access. Kramerbooks is also unique in that it's open 24 hours on weekends, attracting not just the late-night crowd but early-risers, too.

At **Ocooch Books & Libations** in Richland Center, Wisconsin, readers can take home something besides a book to warm the soul. Owner Jodee Hosmanek sells about 40 kinds of wine, 20 Midwest microbrew beers, and 10 kinds of single malt scotch at her bookstore. But you can't drink it in the aisles while you're shopping for the latest bestseller. "The booze is strictly for takeout," Hosmanek laughs. "I'm astounded by how successful it's been. People are very enthusiastic about it."

Hosmanek explains that the florist who occupied the space before her sold wine on the side, and that it only made sense to continue the practice, and even expand on it. She sells more books than libations, she points out, adding that over half of her customers buy both when they stop in.

[www.kramers.com]

EXPANDING VS. SHRINKING

With eight miles of shelf space, the **Strand Bookstore** in New York City is already one of the world's largest used bookstores. But in 2004, the store's owners, Fred Bass and daughter Nancy, announced that the Strand would double its shelf space to 16 miles, making the already huge Greenwich Village landmark a literary colossus.

The store provides "Books by the Foot" for TV shows such as "Saturday Night Live," "The Sopranos" and "Sex and the City," and for movies such as the remakes of "The Stepford Wives" and "The Manchurian Candidate." It also features the largest rare book collection in New York, including many first editions and signed books.

Benjamin Bass, Fred's father, opened the Strand in a different location in 1927 and named it for London's publishing district. It later moved to its current spot at 12th and Broadway, where it occupies five floors of an 11-floor building.

In stark contrast to the Strand is **Danner's Books** in Muncie, Indiana, which was forced in 2004 to decrease its size by a third to make room for a new Subway restaurant. Bookstore owner Susan Danner says the decision was made earlier in the year when she had trouble paying her rent, partially due to the weak local economy. Negotiations with her landlord didn't go very well, she says, leaving her with just two choices: move, or reduce her rent by shrinking the store from 6,000 square feet to 4,000.

Danner made the best of the situation, however. She agreed to do some health- and exercise-related cross-promotion with her new neighbor, as well as with a Curves franchise on the other side of her store. "They're both very interested, and I'm sure I'll sell some healthy-living books or something," Danner says. "We want to think of more things that we can do together."

[Strand Bookstore: www.strandbooks.com]
[Danner's Books: www.dannersbooks.com]

COMMUNITY INVOLVEMENT

Independent booksellers simply have to be involved in the community these days. They can't just put a sign in the window saying "Open for Business," run a few promotions and expect people to line up at their door. They have to be an active part of the local family. There are innumerable ways to do this, and booksellers all over the country are getting creative and finding new ones every day.

One of the most important is to make the bookstore a community gathering place. Many owners offer their cafés or event spaces to local organizations or groups who need a place to meet.

Also, bookstores traditionally have close ties to schools and libraries. Booksellers can partner with them to offer free or discounted books, to support literacy programs, or to co-sponsor events and author readings.

Book donations are a particularly generous type of outreach. Many bookstores give free books to hospitals, nursing homes or senior citizen centers.

They also give them to charities for book drives or raffles. Signed books are great for charitable auctions. Stores can also give away gift certificates, t-shirts, tote bags, coffee mugs and other merchandise, especially if it bears the store's name and logo.

Booksellers also find it worthwhile to join a local business organization such as the chamber of commerce or an independent business alliance. This allows them to get to know other merchants, and it gives them a voice in the business community.

They can also sponsor a kids' sports team, serve on local boards, or give cash donations to important community causes.

Smart booksellers look around their communities to find groups and organizations that may be interested in partnering with them in some way to provide a service or resource. It builds goodwill, and it's also good business sense. The more positive energy a bookstore sends out to the community, the more it gets in return.

CROSS-PROMOTIONS

A lot of indie bookshops are also doing cross-promotions with other businesses.

For example, some stores partner with local movie theaters to offer free tickets. This is especially popular when it's aimed at kids: Buy your child two books and she gets a free ticket to the movies! Theaters are also a good place to hold author readings, and their lobbies make great reception areas.

Some bookstores do cross-promotions with their neighbors: spend $20 on books this week and get a $5 off coupon for the gift shop next door, and vice versa. Three stores all in a row promoting each other – or four or five – are even better.

Similarly, participating in a street festival or block party where all of the merchants in the vicinity hold sales and special events is a terrific way to bring in customers and raise visibility.

Booksellers Associations

Many bookstores belong to national, regional or specialty booksellers associations. The specific goals of each organization varies, but in general their mission is to provide education, information and advocacy to its members. The associations also support free speech, literacy and reading programs.

The American Booksellers Association, founded in 1900, is the national trade organization for independent bookstores. Among its educational efforts are "bookseller schools" for prospective store owners, marketing classes to help members attract more customers, and financial seminars to help booksellers manage their business and plan for the future. The ABA also publishes a widely-read newsletter called Bookselling This Week, which offers the latest industry news and updates from the association.

The ABA's most visible program is Book Sense, a national marketing effort that has proven to be a rising force in the industry and has helped independent bookstores to keep their share of the market. The program's website, BookSense.com, allows its members to sell books online through a combined 2.5 million-title database. Also, the Book Sense gift card, which functions just like the gift cards offered by major retailers, is growing in popularity.

Many bookstores belong to regional booksellers associations. They vary in size and scope, providing news, education and information to their members. They also sponsor regional trade shows where booksellers, publishers, authors and others in the industry can network. Booksellers appreciate the local focus that the regional associations offer through their websites, event calendars, award programs, regional bestseller lists and bookstore listings.

BOOKSTORE TOURISM TIP:

The ABA website, BookWeb.org, includes a search tool that allows visitors to find bookstores by name, city, state or even zip code. Trip planners can also search for bookstores on the regional association websites. All are great resources for anyone planning a bookstore road trip! Keep in mind that not all bookstores belong to a booksellers association, so you may also want to do a Web search. See the section called "How do you research bookstores?"

The major regionals are: the Great Lakes Booksellers Association; the Mid-South Independent Booksellers Association; the Mountains & Plains Booksellers Association; the New Atlantic Independent Booksellers Association; the New England Booksellers Association; the Northern California Independent Booksellers Association; the Pacific Northwest Booksellers Association; the Southeast Booksellers Association; the Southern California Booksellers Association; and the Upper Midwest Booksellers Association.

[See Appendix for association contact information]

INDIE BOOKSTORES IN CYBERSPACE

Independent booksellers have learned that in today's competitive book market, it's crucial to have a website. The Web essentially enables bookstores to be open 24 hours a day. While the physical store is closed, customers can still pay a visit in cyberspace to reserve a book, check the events schedule, read the latest newsletter, see what time a book club is meeting, find out a book's release date, get directions to the store, learn what used or rare books are available, etc.

Likewise, e-mail announcements and electronic newsletters are a quick, relatively cheap and easy way to stay in touch with customers and keep them up-to-date about an author reading, the latest book reviews, a Web-only special, "frequent buyer" programs, and so on.

Plus, thanks to how easy e-commerce has become, an indie store's website can now generate sales from customers in the next town or even from the other side of the world.

READING GROUPS

Reading groups and book clubs have proliferated in the past decade. You can find them in the biggest cities and the smallest towns, from one end of the country to another.

There are countless kinds: Some are devoted to a particular author, others to a specific era or genre. Some serve four-course meals at every meeting, others drink only tea. Some exist only on the Internet. There are mother-daughter reading groups and men's reading groups; bestseller reading groups and science fiction reading groups; reading groups that have been together for 30-plus years, and reading groups that form, break up two weeks later, and regroup again in someone else's house the week after that.

Many clubs are hosted by bookstores that provide space for the gang to meet and can sometimes offer a discount on their selections. Booksellers are also a great resource for picking just the right title to read next. Most will gladly help new groups to form, and can hang up flyers advertising meeting dates and times.

Oprah's Book Club, which started in 1996, is arguably the biggest and best-known reading group. Oprah Winfrey's endorsement virtually guarantees bestseller status for a book. When Winfrey took a 10-month break from the book club business in 2002 and 2003, the morning TV shows quickly jumped in to fill the gap. NBC has its "Today Show Book Club"; "Good Morning America" started one on ABC called "Read This"; and "Live with Regis and Kelly" launched "Reading with Ripa." The CBS "Early Show" also kicked off its "Early Readers' Club" to encourage kids to read over the summer. Then, in 2003, Oprah restarted her book club in a slightly different format, sending classic titles like "The Heart is a Lonely Hunter" by Carson McCullers (1940) and "East of Eden" by John Steinbeck (1952) back onto the bestseller lists.

Although no one has come close to the Winfrey juggernaut, some home-grown reading groups have achieved their own brand of celebrity, like the Pulpwood Queens Book Club. The group was founded by Kathy Patrick, owner of **Beauty and the Book** in Jefferson, Texas – "the only hair salon/bookstore in the country." When the club met for the first time in March 2000, only six people showed up. Now it has over 300 members and 20-plus chapters stretching across the country. In 2003, the

BOOKSTORE TOURISM TIP:

Reading groups and book clubs are an ideal market for bookstore road trips because they're already organized, they like to do things as a group, and they're dedicated to books like few others. If you're in a reading group, think about organizing one for an upcoming activity; or, team up with others in your area to fill a bus. Make it an event!

Pulpwood Queens' original Jefferson chapter helped "Good Morning America" launch its "Read This" program. They've also been featured in Time and Newsweek and on Oprah Winfrey's Oxygen channel. (Patrick herself will soon publish her first book, "The Pulpwood Queen's Guide to Life.")

Many reading groups find other book-related activities to round out their fun, like watching movie adaptations of the books they've read, or attending a lecture on a related topic. Some also enhance their experience by finding out more about a particular culture, or by serving foods that are mentioned in a book.

The popularity of reading groups has been a godsend to booksellers and publishers, who recognize their power to create "buzz" about a book and to influence what gets read.

[Oprah's Book Club: www.oprah.com]
[Beauty & the Book (Pulpwood Queens): www.beautyandthebook.com]

"Keep Austin Weird"

BookPeople in Austin, Texas has become one of the nation's preeminent names in bookselling, not just because of the store's size, literary scope and excellent reputation, but also because its owner Steve Bercu helped to start a "Buy Local" movement that continues to grow across the country.

When a commercial developer announced in 2002 that it planned to open a Borders across the street from BookPeople, Bercu and the owner of a neighboring independent record store resolved to fight the encroachment. The duo printed 5,000 bumper stickers reading "Keep Austin Weird" and handed them out to customers to protest the decision, as well as to discourage the city from providing tax incentives to large corporations that put local merchants out of business. The publicity that resulted prompted Borders to withdraw from the deal (although it officially blamed the weak economy), and a grassroots movement was born.

Fast-forward a year, and what had started as a small, personal demonstration grew into a citywide movement with "Keep Austin Weird" as its rallying cry. People embraced the belief that Austin's quirkiness and independent streak were worth preserving, and the bumper sticker idea (over 100,000 were eventually distributed) morphed into a full-fledged marketing effort. The mayor even appointed a "Keep Austin Weird Task Force," and the city held its first Keep Austin Weird 5K race.

[BookPeople: www.bookpeople.com]
[Keep Austin Weird: www.keepaustinweird.com]

Tattered Cover Book Store, Denver

Each January, Denver's famed Tattered Cover Book Store puts on "Writers Respond to Readers," a day-long seminar featuring four authors who are given free reign to put on whatever kind of program they choose. Tickets to the popular in-store event consistently sell out in about 90 minutes, according to Ellie Hellis, the store's book club coordinator. "We're limited to 120 people, so we wish we could do it several times a year," she says.

Over four sessions — two in the morning and two in the afternoon with a break in between for lunch — the authors generally read from their books and then talk about a related topic or about their writing careers. "The writers can speak about anything they want, and it gives them a chance to discuss their work with their readers," says Hellis.

[www.tatteredcover.com]

Some Ways Independent Bookstores Are Helping to Promote Reading & Literacy

Banned Books Week

Banned Books Week takes place annually during the last week of September. Thousands of organizations participate in this celebration of the freedom to read, including independent bookstores, libraries, schools, colleges, newspapers and magazines. The event reminds Americans not to take the First Amendment for granted and warns of the dangers of censorship. It's sponsored by the American Booksellers Foundation for Free Expression, the American Library Association, the American Society of Journalists and Authors, the Association of American Publishers, and the National Association of College Stores. It's also endorsed by the Library of Congress' Center for the Book. The groups make Banned Book Week kits available to bookstores, schools and libraries, including posters, buttons, t-shirts, and bumper stickers, plus a list of books that have been challenged recently (for example, "The Adventures of Huckleberry Finn" by Mark Twain, "I Know Why the Caged Bird Sings" by Maya Angelou, "Of Mice and Men" by John Steinbeck, and the "Goosebumps" series by R.L. Stine). The event's 2004 theme is "Elect to Read a Banned Book" in observance of the presidential election. [www.ala.org/bbooks]

BookCrossing

BookCrossing is a popular new trend where people are encouraged to read a book and then leave it "out in the wild" for others to find and read before leaving it out for yet another person. The idea, according to co-founder Ron Hornbaker, an American software entrepreneur, is to "make the whole world a library." In August 2003, for example, the people of Manchester, England were asked to look for books everywhere they went in the city, read them, and leave them for someone else. The books – many of which are donated by indie bookstores – are commonly found at street corners, on benches, in waiting rooms, at shopping malls, etc. To take full advantage of the program, members put an ID sticker on each book so participants can visit the BookCrossing.com website, track the book's route and leave their reviews and comments. The site has more than a quarter-million members world-wide. [bookcrossing.com]

Community Wish Lists

Another way bookstores are promoting reading and literacy is by creating "Community Wish List" programs. Booksellers ask local schools and organizations what books they'd like to have and then display the list in the store, stock the titles, and invite customers to purchase them on behalf of the organization.

Get Caught Reading

Many booksellers participate in "Get Caught Reading Month" each May by donating books to schools in their communities. Sponsored by the Association of American Publishers, the national program has been embraced by teachers and librarians as a way to make reading fun for kids. Posters featuring celebrities who have been "Caught Reading" can be found today on many classroom and bookstore walls thanks to the program. [www.getcaughtreading.org]

Independents Week

Held during the first week of July, Independents Week challenges people to shop only at independent businesses for one week. Some stores even encourage customers to take the "Indie Pledge" for the duration. The idea is to raise awareness of the valuable contributions that locally-owned businesses make in their communities, not just economically but in other intangible ways. The initiative is organized by the American Independent Business Alliance (AMIBA), a national outreach organization and resource center for independent businesses. [http://amiba.net]

"One Book" Programs

Nancy Pearl, a librarian, author and former executive director of the Washington Center for the Book, unleashed a phenomenon in 1998 when she created a program called "If All Seattle Read the Same Book." The idea spawned dozens of citywide and community reading programs all around the country, now commonly called "One Book" programs. Many are sponsored and supported by libraries, bookstores, schools and the media. The idea is to get a community's readers to read the same book and participate in a public conversation about it through workshops, reading group meetings, online discussion boards, library and bookstore events, etc. The author of several books, including "Book Lust: Recommended Reading for Every Mood, Moment and Reason," Nancy Pearl has become a "celebrity librarian" for her contribution to the reading community. [www.loc.gov/loc/cfbook/one-book.html]

The Patriot Act

Booksellers and other supporters of free speech have been fighting to amend Section 215 of the "USA Patriot Act," which gives the FBI virtually unlimited power to order bookstores and libraries to turn over customers' records for investigation (the Patriot Act was enacted to fight terrorism). Through the Campaign for Reader Privacy in 2004, booksellers collected close to 200,000 signatures of people who support an amendment to overturn this particular part of Section 215. The effort was sponsored by the American Booksellers Association, the American Library Association, the PEN American Center and the American Booksellers Foundation for Free Expression. It was also supported by dozens of organizations and corporations around the country. Proposed amendments to Section 215 have been unsuccessful as of the publication of this book. [www.readerprivacy.org]

A Bookstore Tourism How-To

A BOOKSTORE TOURISM HOW-TO

Bookstore Adventures for Book Addicts

All of the bookstore trips I've organized so far have been promoted as "adventures" – "Greenwich Village Bookstore Adventure," "Washington, D.C. Bookstore Adventure," "Charlottesville Bookstore Adventure," etc. I emphasize the adventure aspect because that's really what Bookstore Tourism is about: booklovers hitting the road together to discover interesting, fun and unique bookstores that they've never visited before. What could be more exciting to a book addict?

It may seem obvious, but for a bookstore adventure to be successful, you have to plan ahead. Sure, it's fun to wander around unfamiliar neighborhoods with a couple of friends, stopping at bookstores that happen to catch your eye, but if you're organizing a trip for others – and asking them to pay for it – then you need a game plan. You have to decide what you want your trip to be, who's going to go, what you want to do, how you're going to get there, how you're going to publicize it, etc.

This section of the book is arranged Q&A style to guide you through the basic steps of planning a bookstore road trip. I hope it's instructive, and I hope it inspires you to put it to good use. You're invited to build on the idea however you'd like, tweak it to make it your own, or even come up with some completely radical twists.

Bookstore Tourism is a work in progress, so please – feel free to take ownership of it!

Do you have to be some kind of expert to do this?

Do you have to be an expert on the bookselling industry to plan and lead a bookstore trip? A college professor? A travel professional?

None of the above. The only requirements are that you love books and bookstores, and that you have the skills to organize a trip and get other booklovers interested and involved.

Who should consider planning a bookstore road trip?

Any group of booklovers will do, but certain organizations lend themselves particularly well to the idea: reading groups, libraries, schools, colleges, nonprofits, civic organizations, churches, "One Book" programs, book festivals, etc. You don't have to belong to an organization, of course – it can just be you and a bunch of friends or fellow book addicts.

Remember that Bookstore Tourism can go in either direction: Your group can visit the bookstores in another city, or, if your town has some great independent bookshops of its own – and maybe even some literary significance or history – you can attract groups to visit you! Think about the economic possibilities that could result from promoting your community as a "Bookstore Town."

With that in mind, agencies or associations that have a vested interest in tourism and economic development can use Bookstore Tourism as a tool to raise visibility for their community and to promote local merchants. Specifically, chambers of commerce, business associations, tourism bureaus, convention and visitor centers, economic development agencies, or downtown revitalization projects may find it worth exploring.

What's the main purpose of your trip?

Is it strictly for fun, or do you have something educational in mind? Are you hoping to promote your group in some way, or maybe raise funds?

These questions may help you to determine not only who should go along, but also what kind of itinerary you should plan.

Will it cost anything to get started?

Depending on the size of your group, how far you want to travel and what you want to do when you get there, a bookstore trip can be an expensive proposition, to be sure. Or, it could be downright frugal if you really want it to be. Either way, you may need a deposit to reserve a bus, make dinner reservations, get group rates for a tour or event, etc.

If you're lucky enough to be working with a large organization or school, your out-of-pocket expenses (the money you spend before your participants pay) may not be much of an issue. But if your group is small and not particularly well-off, then you'll have to plan your trip on-the-cheap. One solution may be to find a sponsor willing to cover your expenses, even if it's just for a particular part of the trip such as the food, transportation or entertainment. By seeking sponsors – and in return publicizing their assistance both to your group and to the community – you may get enough funding to cover your initial expenses, and maybe even the entire trip. This works especially well if your bookstore adventure is intended as a fundraiser for a nonprofit organization.

Partnering with another organization or business is also a good approach. Combining the resources of two or more groups – your members, customers or contacts – may be the perfect way to launch Bookstore Tourism in your community. For example, the local chamber of commerce can join forces with the library; or maybe the community arts association can team up with a café; a regional magazine with an independent business association; a public radio station with every bookstore in town. Whoever gets involved – whether it's two entities or 10 – should cross-promote the bookstore road trip and each other. Everyone works to make the trip a success, and everyone gets public kudos for helping.

Who are you inviting? How will you handle reservations?

If you're planning your trip for an organization, you'll have to determine if you only want to invite your members, or if you're going to open it up to friends, family, or the entire community. Remember that the more participation you have, the more successful your trip is likely to be.

Also, what's your maximum group size for the trip – 10, 25, 50? Part of this decision depends on the size of your organization and who you're inviting, but also on the mode of transportation you'd like to use. Are you going to charter a motorcoach that seats a few dozen people, or are you going to round up some volunteers to drive their mini-vans? And will the available spots be first-come, first-served?

Which brings us to the next question: How will you handle reservations? Your best bet is to appoint someone to take the phone calls and to keep a list of respondents. Don't forget to set a deadline. You'll also need to decide if everyone needs to pay when they make a reservation, by the deadline, or on the day of the trip. Also, will people be able to pay by cash, check or credit card? Who's going to keep your group's account? You might also want to come up with a clear policy about refunds or cancellations and make everyone aware.

Of course some of these questions may not matter so much if you're planning a trip with just a small group of friends or acquaintances – in which case your only financial concern may be who's going to kick in for coffee and donuts!

Where do you want to go?

Chances are you already have a location (or two or three) in mind. If you're only a half-hour drive from a city with lots of great bookshops, then your choice may be a little more obvious than it is for most. But whether it's a major metropolitan area or a small town out in the boonies, ideally you'll want to consider a location that won't take more than two or three hours to reach, otherwise you'll spend a disproportionate amount of time on the road instead of browsing in bookstores. It's good to remember, too, that anything longer than four hours each way may push most people's tolerance limits, unless your group is particularly adventurous and doesn't mind the travel.

Not sure which towns or cities in your part of the country have great bookstores? See the section called "How do you research bookstores?" (page 66). Also, ask people around your town who are likely to know – fellow book addicts, booksellers, librarians, college professors, etc.

How long do you want the trip to be?

Will it be a day-trip, or are you planning to stay overnight? A weekend? Longer? Most groups will probably be happy with just a day-trip, partly because of the expense of having to spend the night. Still, a two-day bookstore trip can be a lot of fun because it gives you even more time to explore the local bookshops and enjoy other activities such as a guided tour of an author's home or a visit to a site with literary significance. Ask your group how long they'd like to stay.

What day will you go?

Saturdays are great for day-trips. Although some groups, especially retirees, may find that a weekday works better since your destinations may be less crowded than they are on weekends. A Saturday-Sunday overnight trip is a great idea, too. Just be sure to find out the Sunday hours of the places you want to visit.

Also, when you check your calendar, consider what else might be happening in town that day. Planning a trip for the height of tourist season may not be wise, nor do you want to show up in the middle of a St. Patty's parade. However, if a city is holding its annual literary festival at the time of your visit, you could make it the centerpiece of your trip! Plus, if the town you're visiting has a flea market, book fair or library sale going on, you may want to tie into one of those as well.

What time do you want to leave?
When do you want to return?

These questions depend on the distance you plan to travel and how much time you want to spend at your destination. This may seem obvious, but if the city you're planning to visit is three hours away and you'd like to get there by 10 a.m., then you'd have to leave by 7 a.m. at the very latest. But in fact, you'll probably want to allow some extra time in case of delays, or if you group wants to stop for breakfast, so you might want to leave even earlier. For the return trip, if you'd like to be back at your starting point by 11 p.m., then you'd have to hit the road before 8 p.m. So, using this example, you'll ultimately need to consider whether or not 10 hours is enough time (from 10 a.m. to 8 p.m.) for your group to accomplish what it wants to do. Maybe six hours is enough. If you're just 30 minutes from your bookstore town and there are only three shops your group cares to visit, you may only need an afternoon. It's up to you, so do the math and work it out.

What kind of transportation will you use?

If your group is large, you'll almost certainly want to charter a bus or motorcoach. If your group is smaller, you could simply round up some volunteers to drive their mini-vans or cars. Another option, especially if you're working with a public school system, is to arrange for a school bus. If your group happens to be a car, motorcycle or bicycle club of some kind, then your transportation is already built into your plans for the day! (See the section on motorcoaches and travel agents.)

What do you want to do on your trip?

Do you just want to visit bookstores? If so, how many? Would you like to do some other things as well?

It's a good idea to think of some other attractions – literary or not – that are located either at or near your destination (or even on the way, for that matter). For example, did a famous author live in the town you'd like to visit? Are there tours of the author's home? What about a graveyard where a literary figure is buried? Maybe the town you want to visit was the setting for a well-known novel, story or play. Remember, too, that history often ties in nicely with literature, and that a city's historic sites, museums or walking tours could make a worthwhile side-trip for your group.

Towns with these features often take full advantage of their fame or notoriety by building up the local tourist trade around them. Throw in a few great independent bookstores, and what could be better?

What kind of bookstores do you want to visit?

If you're really a book addict – all of them. Seriously, though, aside from the general-interest shops that most of us are familiar with, there are many kinds of specialty bookstores to choose from these days: used, rare, antiquarian, foreign language, religion and spirituality, history, mystery, gay and lesbian, science and technology, and so on. Be on the lookout especially for shops that have a unique niche or personality and reflect the community in some way.

Granted, few cities and towns have a really wide selection of bookstores to choose from. The 20-plus shops in a single square-mile in downtown Manhattan – reflecting just about every taste and interest – is a rarity, to be sure. Your destination may have a college bookstore, two general-interest shops, a co-op, and a gas station with two shelves of discounted bestsellers. Can you make a bookstore road trip out of that? If you're creative enough, sure! (You don't need me to tell you how. Figure it out!)

How do you research bookstores?

If you live close enough to your destination, it may be a simple matter of looking them up in the Yellow Pages. If you're not nearby, however, there are other, fairly simple ways to find them on the World Wide Web.

The website for the American Booksellers Association, www.bookweb.org, has a fantastic search tool at the bottom of the page that allows you to look for bookstores by name, city, state or zip code. From there, you can usually click on a link to a particular bookshop's website. Remember, though, that not all bookstores are members of the ABA, so you may want to keep looking.

You can also try SuperPages.com, an excellent resource that lets you browse the national Yellow or White Pages by keyword (e.g. "books" or "bookstores"), business name, city and state. For example, a search for bookstores in Omaha, Nebraska yielded 75 booksellers, including 16 used and rare shops, nine religion and seven children's.

Also, try getting on Google, Yahoo, or one of the other major search engines. For example, I typed in "Boulder" and "bookstores" and came up with several different websites with lists of bookstores in Boulder, Colorado. From there it's often just another click – or sometimes one more search using the specific store name – to get to the shop's website, or at least to its address and telephone number. If you study a few of these sites, it's fairly easy to compile a list of all the bookstores in town. (Remember that the Web is an inexact science, so you'll have to take the good with the bad and sort through to see what you can find. You can narrow or broaden your search terms, try other words like "booksellers," etc. If you're not the most Web-savvy person, ask someone to help you.)

Another thing to think about is where the bookstores you want to visit are located within the city or town. Are you going to travel as a group from store to store, or will everyone be on their own to browse all day? Are the stores within walking distance of each other? Or will you have to load everyone back into your vehicles at some point and drive them across town to another location?

If your group is planning to visit only three or four bookstores in a small- or medium-sized town, your job is a lot easier. But if you're targeting a major metropolitan area with a dozen or more bookstores spread pretty far apart, then you may have to do some creative planning. Are any of them grouped in the same vicinity? If so, you could do one part of town in the morning and another in the afternoon.

Should you scout the bookstores ahead of time?

As far as I'm concerned, this is one of the immutable laws of Bookstore Tourism: You must do a reconnaissance trip!

In other words, you really should do the leg-work and visit the stores on your list if you're not already familiar with them; that way you avoid any surprises and your group doesn't come away disappointed. It's a good idea to go weeks or even months in advance to look them over, confirm their location, double-check their hours of operation, etc. And truthfully, for anyone planning a bookstore adventure, this may actually be one of the most enjoyable parts of the job because you get to visit the stores before everyone else! (Keep in mind, too, that you can scout bookstores during your regular travels – it doesn't just have to be to reconnoiter for a road trip. Then again, if you're a book addict, you probably already do that anyway!)

When you go to check out the stores, take along your list, with addresses, and a city map so you can mark down exactly where they are. This comes in handy for the map that you'll probably create for your group, whether it's a simple drawing you'll make on your own or a detailed street map you'll base on a published one. Also, take along a notepad so you can jot down a description of each store, along with some of its special features and your general impressions, and then include a short blurb for each shop on your trip map or brochure.

Here are some examples from my Greenwich Village brochure:

- **Shakespeare & Co.:** 716 Broadway. An intimate bookshop with a collection equal to any chain store. Great selection of art, theatre, film, and crime books. Be sure to check out the basement, too! Opens at 10 a.m.
- **Skyline Books:** 13 W. 18th St. Specializes in rare 1st editions, signed copies and great finds for serious collectors or casual browsers alike. It's everything you'd expect an excellent secondhand bookstore to be. Opens at 10 a.m.
- **Three Lives & Company:** 154 W. 10th St. A tiny Greenwich Village institution with a gigantic literary reputation. Many of the city's top writers, agents, editors and publishers shop here. Browsing is encouraged. The staff is friendly and helpful. Opens at 11 a.m.

What qualities should you look for in a bookstore?

It really depends on your personal taste, but I always say that the top requirements for any worthwhile bookstore are:

1. a wide selection;
2. a friendly atmosphere;
3. a helpful staff; and
4. overall good vibes.

Does this mean you shouldn't let your group visit a store that doesn't match these descriptions? Certainly not. Some of the best bookstores are totally disorganized, have snooty employees, and won't let you use the bathroom unless you buy something. It's all part of the adventure. (You wouldn't miss riding to the bottom of the Grand Canyon just because your donkey attracts flies, would you?)

Would you like to attend an author reading or book-signing?

If you plan your trip well in advance, you may be able to coordinate it for a day that an author reading or book-signing is scheduled. Or, as the date of your trip gets closer, you may find out that an author has been scheduled for an appearance in the city you're planning to visit, in which case you can simply let everyone know. This is precisely what happened on one of our New York trips when the humorist/cartoonist Jules Pfeiffer happened to be appearing at **Books of Wonder**. I announced the news to our group on the way to the city, and several of our participants stopped to see him and got him to autograph his new children's book.

Still another option is to ask the booksellers you plan to visit if they can arrange an author visit specifically for your group, either at the bookstore or at another point in your travels. Remember, too, that a reading or book-signing doesn't require a bestselling author or a household name; the booksellers you're working with can probably recommend a terrific regional or local author who would be perfect for your group and more than happy to visit with you, read from her work, and sign your books.

Do bookstores hold non-literary events?

Many bookstores have events that aren't necessarily book-related but can easily be tied in to specific titles they offer, such as demonstrations (cooking, massage, sculpture, martial arts), expert presentations (a local matchmaking service representative on dating, a child psychologist on back-to-school jitters), and kids' activities (arts and crafts, theater), etc. These events are fairly easy for the bookstore to create, and they get customers excited about things that are informational and fun. Consider asking the booksellers on your list about them as you're planning your trip, and then let your participants know what's going on.

How do you work with booksellers?

My experience so far with the booksellers on our trips has been fantastic. They love the Bookstore Tourism concept, and they want to see it succeed. They're always happy to see our groups arrive (they recognize our participants by the brochures), and they've always been very accomodating.

It's a good idea to write, e-mail or phone the booksellers on your list to let them know you're coming. If your group is large and everyone will be free to browse the bookstores on their own, be sure to let the booksellers know that you won't be arriving all at the same time (many bookshops are very small and could never accommodate more than 20-25 people). If the store is large, though, the owner may be overjoyed to have a crowd pay a visit, especially for an author reading or some other special event.

Some booksellers will offer refreshments, or a place for your participants to leave their books temporarily while they continue shopping elsewhere. If they offer, great. If not, don't be pushy. Remember that they have a business to run, and that one of the main reasons for your trip is to support independent booksellers, not to make them play host to your organization.

Don't forget to tell your booksellers who you are when you arrive, and give them a copy of your brochure if you haven't sent one ahead of time. Chances are, when they see your group coming through the door, they'll want to see you and other bookstore tourists again very soon.

Where are you going to eat?

Do you want to dine together, or will everyone eat on their own? For an all-day trip with a two- or three-hour drive each way, it might work best to stop somewhere in the morning for a quick breakfast at a diner or fast-food joint. Depending on your itinerary, you could let everyone have lunch on their own, especially if there's a good selection of cafés and restaurants within walking distance. Later you could have the group meet up again for dinner, perhaps somewhere a little more upscale. Any variation on this scenario will do, of course, from eating a brown-bag lunch on the bus to having a caterer serve you tea on the lawn of a famous novelist's home!

The dinners we've had at Spirito Grill in the Sheraton Suites in Weehawken, New Jersey have been wonderful. The restaurant is located on the Hudson River waterfront with an incredible view of the Manhattan skyline. Our groups always use the occasion (at my suggestion) to brag about the great books they found that day and to compare notes on the stores they visited. It's a bonding experience for booklovers, and it's a lot of fun.

Is there anything interesting or fun you can plan for the ride?

If you charter a bus, you might consider doing a presentation of some kind on the way to your destination. A literary topic would be appropriate, of course, or you could talk about subjects relating to your group or organization. You could have a guest speaker, reports from a couple of members, announcements from your chairman, a group discussion on a particular topic, etc. (I'm not recommending that you do ALL of these things. Your bus driver will be glad to lend you the microphone, but he won't want an entire cast of characters taking turns at the front of the aisle.)

As for your entertainment options during the drive, most motorcoaches today have a DVD or VHS player, with TV monitors every few rows. They also have reading lights, which could come in handy if anyone in your group is chomping at the bit to read their new finds on the way home.

Here are some excellent bookstore-related movies that I highly recommend for viewing on your trip:

- "84 Charing Cross Road," starring Anne Bancroft and Anthony Hopkins (1987) – An American writer corresponds with the proprietor of an antiquarian bookshop in London over several decades (based on a true story).
- "Notting Hill," starring Julia Roberts and Hugh Grant (1999) – The owner of a London travel bookshop falls in love with an American actress.
- "You've Got Mail," starring Tom Hanks and Meg Ryan (1998) – The owner of a large bookstore chain and the owner of a small Manhattan children's bookstore meet and fall in love over the Internet. (He also puts her out of business in the process!)

How will you publicize your trip?

You'll probably want to publicize your trip as soon as possible so you can start taking reservations. There are a lot of different ways to get the word out, most of them either free or cheap. Decide the most effective means to reach your target audience and take full advantage of it.

Whatever you send out or post, make sure you include the basic facts as well as any important details. At the very least, you'll want to mention the purpose of the trip, date, time, pickup and dropoff location, destination(s), special features, cost, and any sponsors or partners with whom you're working. Somewhere in your text you might also want to describe the basic idea behind Bookstore Tourism, which is to promote and support independent bookstores by marketing them as a travel destination.

Here are some examples of how you can publicize your bookstore trip:

- Post an announcement on your organization's website.
- Put an article or ad in your newsletter.
- Send a news release to your local media.
- Put up a flyer around town where your target audience will see it.
- Ask your newspaper to run a couple of lines on its community event page.
- Get your radio or TV station to run a public service announcement.
- Put a small blurb on your local cable access channel.
- If you can afford it, place an ad in a local newspaper or magazine.
- Ask other organizations to announce it.
- Include the details in all of the communications material your organization sends out, including e-mails.
- Don't forget phone calls and word-of-mouth!

Here's a sample blurb from one of my trips:

Charlottesville Bookstore Adventure
Saturday, November 6, 2004
If you're passionate about books, you won't want to miss this visit to historic Charlottesville, Virginia – one of the best "bookstore towns" on the East Coast! Your bus will leave the Lebanon Campus at 5 a.m., make a stop at the Wildwood Campus in Harrisburg at 5:45 a.m., and then proceed to Virginia, stopping along the way for a fast food breakfast and arriving in Charlottesville around 10:30 a.m. During the drive, your guide, Larry Portzline, will offer a presentation on current trends in the bookselling industry. Your map for the day includes numerous downtown bookstores to browse at your leisure – from current bestsellers to rare finds, from kids' titles to the unusual – plus great used bookshops. The quaint Main Street pedestrian mall also boasts plenty of great cafés for lunch and shops for additional browsing on your own. The group will meet again at 5 p.m. for dinner and a visit by a special guest author. A treat for the ride home will be the film "84 Charing Cross Road," starring Anne Bancroft and Anthony Hopkins, whose long-distance friendship is fueled by a passion for old books. Cost includes bus, guide, and dinner. Quick breakfast and lunch are on your own.

Can you get your local media to cover your bookstore trip?

Consider asking your local newspaper or radio or TV station to run a story about your bookstore trip. Local media outlets are always interested in covering topics that are new and unique, and Bookstore Tourism certainly fits the bill. Your newspaper may be able to run a news release to help you publicize your trip, or you might even be able to get a reporter or TV crew to go along for the ride and file a report about it.

Here's a sample news release that you can use as the basis for your own. Just replace the capitalized words with your own information, and add any other details you want to include:

For Immediate Release
TODAY'S DATE

YOUR ORGANIZATION to Host
"CITY Bookstore Adventure"

YOUR TOWN – Attention, booklovers! Hop on the bus for a day of literary fun with the first-ever "CITY Bookstore Adventure," sponsored by YOUR ORGANIZATION.

This unique road trip will take place between TIME a.m. and TIME p.m. on DATE, and will feature NUMBER independent bookstores, including: NAMES OF STORES. There will be a mid-day break for lunch "on your own" during a stop at PLACE.

During the trip, PERSON will offer a presentation on TOPIC. ANOTHER PERSON will DO SOMETHING ELSE. LIST ANY OTHER SPECIAL HIGHLIGHTS.

"This is an unprecedented opportunity for those who share a love of books, bookstores and reading to join in a spirit of camaraderie and just plain fun," said ORGANIZER, TITLE of YOUR ORGANIZATION. "ANY-THING ELSE YOU WANT TO SAY."

Tickets for the day-long tour are $PRICE, and include transportation, HIGHLIGHT #1 and HIGHLIGHT #2. Seating is limited and will be offered on a first-come, first-served basis.

To make a reservation, please respond by DEADLINE. For additional information, contact PERSON at PHONE or E-MAIL.

# # #

Media Contact: PERSON, PHONE, etc.

What kind of materials should you create for the trip?

Depending on the size of the city or town you plan to visit and the extent of your travels, you may want to give everyone a map of the area with all of the stores marked clearly, plus any other locations you need to highlight such as the starting point of a walking tour or the restaurant where the group will have dinner.

A brochure with a map provides an excellent guide for your participants. You can go all out and have a graphic artist design it for you, but these days it's easier than ever to get on your computer, download a template and do it yourself. Some possibilities for content are the basic facts about your organization, a few graphics or photos, acknowledgments and thanks, sponsor or partner information, etc.

If the town you're visiting isn't very large, you can probably design a fairly simple street map for your brochure, but if you're visiting a big city, you may want to create something more detailed. Depending on how many bookstores are on your list, you may want to number them and include corresponding descriptions next to the map. The descriptions could include the store name, address, types of books they carry, phone number, website, hours of operation, etc., plus your general impressions from your reconnaissance trip. (Refer back to the examples in "Should you scout the bookstores ahead of time?")

You can hand out the brochures as everyone gets on the bus. Be sure to have extras to give to the booksellers on your list, and also for some of your participants who'll want to give one to a friend (it's great advertising for future trips!). You can view the brochures I've used for my trips at www.bookstoretourism.com.

Also, consider creating a survey that you can distribute on the ride home and ask everyone to fill it out. This will give you some valuable feedback about how your group liked the trip and help you plan for the next one.

Here's a survey that I've used for my trips. Feel free to adapt it however you want:

THANKS FOR JOINING US TODAY!

We hope you had a great time on our Greenwich Village Bookstore Adventure!

We're glad you could join us, and we hope you'll come again.

More trips are in the works, so please keep an eye out for future news!

We'd appreciate it if you could take a few minutes to fill out this feedback form and tell us about your experience today – what you enjoyed, any suggestions you may have, what we could do better, etc.

Names are optional – just hand in the form before you leave for home tonight.

Thanks again for taking part in our adventure!

Happy reading!

Please circle your responses or fill in the blanks:

1. **Overall, I would rate my experience today as:**
   Wonderful   Good   Okay   Disappointing   Awful

2. **The bus service was:**
   Wonderful   Good   Okay   Disappointing   Awful

3. **The bookstore choices were:**
   Wonderful   Good   Okay   Disappointing   Awful

4. **The dinner at _____ was:**
   Wonderful   Good   Okay   Disappointing   Awful

5. **How many bookstores did you visit today?** ____

6. **How many books did you buy?** ____

7. **What did you like best about the trip?** ____

8. **Do you have any suggestions for future bookstore trips?**
   _____

9. **Would you recommend this trip to a friend?**   Yes   No

Thanks for sharing your day with us!

What should you do when you arrive at your destination?

If you charter a bus, it's a good idea to plan where you'd like your group to be dropped off and picked up so you can tell your driver ahead of time. He or she may be able to take you to the exact spot upon arrival, but depending on traffic, the neighborhood and other circumstances, you may have to shoot for an approximate location.

When you arrive, tell your group exactly where they are, suggest that they write it down or mark it on the map, and point out an easily recognizable landmark so they'll know approximately where you're supposed to meet again (this applies whether you're splitting up or staying together, because you never know when someone might run astray). Also, remind everyone about your game plan – what you're doing and when, where you're eating, what time you're leaving, what you'll do on the drive home, etc.

You might also consider having a designated place where your group can drop off their books for safekeeping if they'd like. Bags full of books can get very heavy when you're doing a lot of walking, so ask one or two of the booksellers on your list if they would allow your group to drop off their bags temporarily so they can keep on shopping. Then, give your group that option and remind them when you arrive that they are responsible for going back and picking up their books before the group is scheduled to meet again.

Why charter a bus?

There are many advantages to hiring a motorcoach company to transport your group to and from your destination: They do the driving so you don't have to worry about traffic, maps, tolls, parking and other hassles; they offer door-to-door convenience; they offer security and peace-of-mind; and, you can relax in comfort during the drive, enjoy the scenery, watch a movie, sleep or socialize. Also, it's easier than rounding up a half-dozen volunteers with mini-vans!

How do you find and choose a motorcoach company?

A good place to start is the Yellow Pages. You can also ask friends, neighbors, relatives or co-workers for recommendations. Also, the websites of the American Bus Association (www.buses.org) and the United Motorcoach Association (www.uma.org) – the motorcoach industry's two major trade organizations – have search engines allowing you to search for an operator by name, city or state.

Motorcoaches come in different sizes, generally ranging from 47-seat to slightly larger 55-seat models. It's not absolutely necessary for you to fill the bus, although the more people you have, the easier it will be to afford. Most motorcoaches are equipped with TV monitors every few rows, a VCR or DVD, a stereo system, a microphone and PA system, a restroom, reclining seats, air conditioning, tinted windows, luggage compartments and reading lights. Depending on the company, the rate you'll pay will be based on the number of passengers, the size of the bus and/or your estimated mileage.

You'll want to be able to give the company some details about the trip when you call: how many people are going, what time you want to leave and return, where you'd like to be picked up and dropped off, your basic itinerary, any special activities or events you're considering, and who will act as your group's contact person. When you call, be sure to ask the price and how it's determined, what it includes, if a deposit is required, about the company's cancellation policy, whether the bus is equipped with the above items, about the company's policy on a gratuity for the driver, and anything else you may want to know.

What do you need to know about working with a bus driver?

The vast majority of motorcoach drivers are professionals through and through. They're friendly, courteous, experienced, knowledgable, and they'll do whatever they can to make your trip as successful as it can be.

The drivers in your region probably know their way around by heart. They know the towns and cities, which routes to take and which to avoid, the best attractions, some good restaurants along the way, etc. And thanks to cell phones, they're only a call away from you and from their company should the need arise, so be sure to exchange numbers.

If you have a preferred route to your destination, or if you have any minor changes in your itinerary, be sure to let the driver know as soon as possible. As long as the request is reasonable, he or she will be happy to accommodate. After depositing your group at your destination, the driver will park the bus and find something to do until he or she is needed again. Some drivers read, some snooze, others do some sightseeing themselves.

If a tip for the driver isn't included in the cost of your trip, be sure to pass around an envelope during the ride home and ask everyone to contribute a dollar or two. Also, if you're going to eat as a group at any point during the day, invite the driver to join you and make sure the cost of the meal is covered, either by your group or by the restaurant (some establishments offer complimentary meals to motorcoach drivers).

Should you hire a travel agent, and how do you choose one?

If your trip is fairly routine, not terribly far away, and you're somewhat experienced in making travel arrangements, you may be able to book it yourself. Conversely, if your trip involves a large group, multiple stops or a tricky itinerary, a knowledgeable travel agent can make your planning go much easier.

Here are some reasons why a travel agent may be just the ticket (sorry):

- They're knowledgeable and experienced.
- They offer one-stop shopping for all your needs.
- They can find the information you need quickly and easily.
- They can offer recommendations – including extras you never would have considered on your own.
- They can book just about everything – your bus, meals, tickets, accommodations, special activities, etc.
- They can find the best prices.
- They can tailor your arrangements to fit your personal interests, special needs or budget concerns.
- They often specialize in certain kinds of travel.

Most people are careful when choosing an electrician or a long distance telephone company, so you ought to be careful about choosing a travel agent, too. A good place to start is by asking a friend, relative or co-worker for a recommendation. Failing that, check your phone book or do a search on the Web.

The best travel agents are friendly, reputable, detail-oriented, and a wealth of information. If you don't find these qualities in the first travel agent you go to, you may want to shop around. Ultimately you'll want to find someone who will happily work with you to determine your group's goals and needs, and will strive to meet them efficiently and affordably.

What can go wrong?

Anything could go wrong, conceivably. Your bus could get a flat tire; an author reading could be cancelled; a dinner could be terrible; a thunderstorm could last all afternoon. All you can do is prepare for these eventualities – if not literally at least mentally – and be ready to act if disaster strikes.

One of the most common concerns when traveling with a group is what to do if someone doesn't show up when you're ready to depart; or perhaps worse, if someone doesn't come back to your meeting spot for the ride home. The reality is that if you're dealing with a few dozen people who have paid good money to go on your trip, and someone isn't where they're supposed to be at the appointed time, you can't in good conscience keep everyone else waiting. Your best bet is to make clear to everyone, when they reserve a seat and again during the trip, that the bus will leave when scheduled. In other words, if they're not there, they'll be left behind and won't receive a refund.

Sometimes, though, circumstances arise that are no one's fault, and may require some quick thinking and action. On one of our trips, for example, we nearly left a woman behind during a breakfast stop in Allentown, Pennsylvania. Fortunately the woman had a great sense of humor and recognized that the mishap was a fluke!

The problem actually started early that morning when our driver realized there was a slight mechanical problem with the bus. Not wanting to take any chances, he called his company and asked them to provide a new bus in

Allentown, where we were also supposed to switch drivers (motorcoach companies sometimes do this to relieve drivers who are ready to come off duty, much in the same way that airlines switch pilots). When we arrived at the restaurant, we discovered that it too was having mechanical difficulties and was not yet open. Some members of our party immediately decided to walk to a nearby donut shop, and everyone cheerfully followed suit.

Problem solved, right? Not quite.

Following the bus-and-driver switch, our new driver offered to give a lift to those of us who hadn't yet made it across the street to the donut shop. What no one realized at the time was that one of our female participants was already on her way back from the donut shop, and that she had no way of knowing that the bus wouldn't be there when she returned. Needless to say, we were one head short for our headcount a little while later, and quickly drove back to the restaurant to pick up our wayward friend, who by this time was thinking about hailing a taxi to the nearest Greyhound terminal.

On another trip, just moments after I stood at the front of the bus and began my presentation, a woman in the second seat became ill. She apparently hadn't realized until that very moment that the flu symptoms she'd been experiencing all morning might somehow interfere with her enjoyment of our trip. I was aware that something was amiss but continued with my presentation, only slightly distracted by the unpleasant faces of those around her.

These are just a couple of examples of what can go wrong. Admittedly, they're pretty mild. So far we've been lucky, and I wish you the same kind of luck!

What ideas do you have for bookstore road trips?

Write to me and let me know, and I may include you in the next expanded edition of this book! See the Afterword for details.

Great Towns for Bookstore Tourists

GREAT TOWNS FOR BOOKSTORE TOURISTS

Some of the most common questions I'm asked about Bookstore Tourism are:

- Where are the best bookstore towns?
- Which cities have the highest concentration of indie bookshops?
- What small towns have a surprising number of bookstores?
- Are there places that have literary significance with maybe just a handful of bookstores worth visiting?

Unfortunately, answering these questions to the extent I would like would require the creation of a Bookstore Atlas of the United States (and possibly of the world for international travelers). I know that sounds like a great idea, but can you imagine the work involved? It would take a lot more research than just looking up towns on the Web or opening the Yellow Pages or finding addresses on a map. You'd have to *go,* and that could take a lifetime. Plus there's the problem of bookstores closing, or moving, or changing owners, so it wouldn't stay accurate for long. (On the other hand, regional and city guides would be much easier to produce, and are something I'm considering for future Bookstore Tourism books.)

To make do, though, I'm offering here a short sampling of "Great Towns for Bookstore Tourists" – mostly in the U.S., but starting off with a couple others that I think you should know about for very different reasons, as you'll see. I've also included a town that's known for a particular book, a city that's known for a particular bookstore, and a community that's known for a particular author – all of which would make fantastic destinations for your bookstore road trips!

The list is limited, obviously. And that atlas idea is starting to sound better and better.

Hay-on-Wye, Wales: "The Town of Books"

A tiny village in central Wales called Hay-on-Wye has earned a worldwide reputation as the "The Town of Books." Its annual festival is one of Britain's top literary gatherings, with 80,000 visitors crowding in for the carnival-like revelry.

Hay earned its nickname because it reportedly has more bookstores per capita than any other town in the world. Its 39 bookshops serve just 1,500 residents – one bookstore for every 38 people. Hay also has pubs, restaurants, inns and a medieval castle, making it a charming escape for any literary traveler.

The town's success is largely due to the efforts of Richard Booth, an eccentric native of the area who graduated from Oxford and later became a book dealer. In the 1960s, Booth decided that if Hay could become "a town full of bookshops," it might become an international attraction (Bookstore Tourism to the extreme, you might say). In 1977, Booth declared independence for Hay and appointed himself "King," a stunt that brought worldwide attention to the village. Later, when a study conducted by a Scottish University showed that Hay's economic effect on the region was enormous, its "bookstore town" model was copied by communities in France, Belgium and the Netherlands.

The Hay Festival of Literature is held each spring.

[www.hayfestival.com]

Charing Cross Road, London

Sadly, not all bookstore towns are thriving. In fact, one of the most renowned bookselling districts in the world has virtually disappeared. I've included it in this list because the same thing could happen here in the U.S. if we let it.

Charing Cross Road is one of London's most famous streets, and for decades was recognized as a literary mecca for its numerous used, rare and specialty bookshops. But in 2001 and 2002, rents in the neighborhood skyrocketed suddenly as landlords tried to cash in on the area's name and popularity. Londoners were outraged, calling the rent increases "punitive" and blaming the situation on greed and "homogenous" over-commercialization. Nevertheless, the bookstores started closing one by one and were quickly replaced by souvenir shops and national chain stores.

To add insult to injury, the most celebrated address on the street, 84 Charing Cross Road, was taken over by an "All Bar One" franchise – a national pub chain that many Brits have blamed for the decline of the traditional English pub. The building was made famous in Helene Hanff's 1970 novel "84 Charing Cross Road" (based on a true story), and by the 1986 film adaptation starring Anne Bancroft and Anthony Hopkins.

The closings led to public predictions that the same thing would happen to other London neighborhoods that are known by their individual personalities, by their quirks, and by the longstanding merchants – including the independent bookshops – that have shaped the local identity.

As one local put it, "In the world of rent, there's no sentiment." (The [London] Independent, December 8, 2001)

Georgetown and Dupont Circle, Washington, D.C.

It would be a wild stretch to put Washington, D.C.'s funky and fun Georgetown neighborhood on the same par with Charing Cross Road, but the rapid disappearance of bookstores in this "small town" within the nation's capital certainly invites comparison.

A personal anecdote:

For my girlfriend Deb and me, one of the most enjoyable aspects of planning bookstore road trips has been our reconnaissance missions to the area we plan to visit, to see the bookstores firsthand and to get the flavor of the community. This usually involves studying maps, checking locations, jotting down bookstore descriptions, sampling the local pubs and cafés, etc. Usually I bring a good city map on which I've marked each bookstore's approximate location based on the results of an address search on MapQuest.com (another great resource for anyone planning a bookstore trip!). Then, as I find each store, I mark the more precise location on my city map so I can get it right when I design my own for the trip brochure.

Deb and I had already visited Georgetown's bookstores on several occasions when we returned in January 2004 to scout an upcoming trip. The wind-chill that day was brutal to say the least, hovering around zero degrees. But we had a long list of bookshops to visit, and I had my maps and notepad at the ready to do the necessary research.

The first two bookstores were exactly where they were supposed to be, but they hadn't yet opened for the day, so we figured we'd walk a little further and come back later on.

That's when our trip turned into The Twilight Zone.

The next shop on our list wasn't there anymore, which was really disappointing since it had been owned by the author Larry McMurtry ("Texasville," "Lonesome Dove," "Terms of Endearment"), and we'd really enjoyed it the last time we'd visited.

As we trudged up to the next address, our legs now completely numb, we found that it, too, no longer contained a bookstore. It was now a hair salon. Next address, a realtor. The next, empty.

I was panic-stricken, imagining my phone call to the college sponsoring the bookstore trip, telling them that the display ad they'd just included in a circular mailed to every residence in four counties was now fiction itself.

We soldiered on, praying for a miracle. Some of the bookshops were still open, thankfully, but as wonderful as they are, it didn't seem enough to warrant a group of 45 booklovers getting up early, riding two hours each way, getting home late, and paying good money to do so.

Deb wasn't sure if I was shivering from the cold or the onset of a mental collapse. More than half of the 14 bookstores on my list were gone. We stood on the street, asking each other what could have happened since the last time we'd visited just months before.

To make a long story short – thank God for Dupont Circle.

Just one neighborhood over, not half a mile from where we were standing, were some of the most impressive bookstores we've ever visited. Being the good planner that I am (although Deb has a less polite term for it), I had my Dupont Circle list and maps with me, too; so we took a quick drive around, made sure the shops were still open, and wound up having a fantastic time several months later with a group that was positively thrilled with our combined Georgetown / Dupont Circle Bookstore Adventure.

The end of this story isn't totally happy, however...

We were relieved that we saved the trip, obviously – but we still don't know what happened to all of those great bookstores in Georgetown.

Greenwich Village, New York City

Greenwich Village is the birthplace of Bookstore Tourism. It's exactly what I had in mind when I came up with the idea in that first conversation with Don Koones at Harrisburg Area Community College.

To be accurate, though, not all of the bookstores on our New York brochure are in Greenwich Village; some are just over the border in Chelsea, Soho, and other surrounding neighborhoods (if you want to know precisely where the dividing lines are, ask a New Yorker, who will be all too glad to educate you, I'm sure). Either way, there are 20-plus independent bookstores in and around Greenwich Village, all within a single square-mile and easily within walking distance of each other. There are some general-interest booksellers, but there are also plenty of specialty and niche shops to satisfy just about any reader's needs or interests. Few cities in the world can claim such an amazing concentration of bookshops.

I've described a few of them throughout this book, but here's a small sampling of the others just to give you a taste: there's Books of Wonder, one of the best children's bookstores you're likely to find anywhere; Lectorum Books, operated by the nation's oldest and largest Spanish book translator and distributor; Partners & Crime, a casual basement shop specializing in mysteries; Skyline Books, with its amazing collection of used, first-edition and signed books; St. Mark's Bookshop, which helps to define the word eclectic; and Three Lives & Company, a small shop that's frequented by many writers and artists.

Why so many great bookstores in one small area? Because the local culture requires it. The neighborhood is loaded with history. It's very artistic and quirky. It's academic. It's intellectual and free-thinking. People in this kind of community crave intellectual stimulation, and they know their bookstores are at the center of that need.

More towns should be so lucky.

Charlottesville, Virginia

Charlottesville, Virginia is one of the lucky ones. It has all of the attributes listed above for Greenwich Village, but it couldn't be more different in other ways. The pace is much slower, for one thing, and its southern charm is evident everywhere you look. It's the home of Thomas Jefferson, Monticello, and the University of Virginia. It's also host to the Virginia

Festival of the Book, a five-day celebration held each March that draws thousands of visitors and dozens of authors to its free readings, seminars and panel discussions. [www.vabook.org]

Charlottesville's famous cobblestone pedestrian mall, on what used to be the town's main thoroughfare, is lined with quaint shops and cafés, as well as some terrific bookstores. The New Dominion Bookshop, for example, is the oldest independent bookseller in Virginia. It has one of the most cozy, intimate event spaces you'll ever see in a bookstore: a wide balcony, up the staircase and at the back of the shop, with a wooden floor and a wall of windows that give it the feel of a classroom in an old schoolhouse. The space can fit about 30 tightly, and maybe a few more if they squeeze onto the other steps leading to the top floor. During an author reading, it's easy to transport yourself back to 1924 when the store first opened, sitting in the same spot, listening to the rain tap lightly on the windows.

There are at least a couple dozen other bookstores in and around town to suit a wide variety of tastes – from current bestsellers to rare finds, from kids' titles to the unusual – plus some wonderful used bookshops.

Charlottesville is also the home of several well-known authors, including John Grisham and Rita Mae Brown, as well as Oscar-winning actress Sissy Spacek, so you never know who you might run into while you're browsing for books.

"Midnight" in Savannah, Georgia

If towns are going to be known for anything, they could do a lot worse than being renowned for a wildly popular novel. These days, visitors to Savannah, Georgia probably know the city better for "The Book," as it's called locally, than its azaleas, its historic architecture and its old-fashioned hospitality.

"The Book" is John Berendt's fact-based novel "Midnight in the Garden of Good and Evil," considered a modern classic by many. A murder mystery set against an engaging portrait of Savannah, the story has caused a major travel boom in the city since its publication in 1994. The 1997 film version directed by Clint Eastwood also did its part to attract visitors.

What used to be a quiet town on the Atlantic coast has gone through a renaissance thanks in large part to "Midnight," with new hotels, restored buildings and upscale stores now dotting the streets. Two of Savannah's booksellers – Esther Shaver, of E. Shaver Bookseller, and John Duncan, co-owner of V. and J. Duncan Antique Maps and Prints – have sold thousands of copies of the book, and continue to sell more every day, mostly to tourists who simply have to pick one up while they're in town.

"Midnight" broke publishing records by spending more than four years on the New York Times Bestseller List. The Savannah Morning News called it "the biggest thing to hit the city since William Tecumseh Sherman."

San Francisco's City Lights

It should come as no surprise that San Francisco, one of the most cerebral and open-minded cities in the nation, has a multitude of independent book-shops of every size and kind. But among all of its bookshops, City Lights Bookstore is probably the most famous. Co-founded by the writer Lawrence Ferlinghetti, City Lights celebrated its 50th anniversary as an icon of free speech in 2003. A haven for beatniks in the 1950s and a hangout for hippies in the '60s, it's now one of the most visited tourist destinations in San Francisco (the city made it an official landmark in 2000).

City Lights is also a publisher, having printed some of the most important works of Beat Generation writers Jack Kerouac, William S. Burroughs and Allen Ginsberg. Ferlinghetti had his first brush with notoriety in the mid-1950s when he was tried for obscenity for publishing Ginsberg's long-form poem "Howl." The landmark censorship case thrust City Lights into the national consciousness, and although Ferlinghetti was acquitted in 1957, he

TRIVIA:

According to a 2003 study by the U.S. Bureau of Labor and Statistics, San Francisco leads the country in book sales per capita, with the average resident spending $266 on books each year. The same study noted that San Franciscans also spend more money on alcohol than any other population in the country, at $744 a year per person. When these results were announced, the San Francisco Chronicle reported that there was a correlation between the two facts and said, "There are more well-read drinkers in San Francisco than anywhere else in the land."
(Source: "San Francisco is No. 1 – in Books and Booze," Steve Rubenstein, San Francisco Chronicle, May 16, 2003)

would be raided multiple times by federal authorities for selling "immoral" or "lewd" material.

Part of the store's golden anniversary celebration included a packed event in New York City, featuring writers and performers who read from the works of Ferlinghetti, Ginsberg and others.

Elmira, New York: Mark Twain's Summer Home

Although Mark Twain (Samuel Clemens) and his family lived in Hartford, Connecticut, they spent more than 20 summers with his wife Olivia's relatives on Quarry Farm in Elmira, New York. In 1874, the family built an octagonal study for Twain a short distance from the farmhouse, on a knoll overlooking the Chemung Valley. It was there that Twain worked on some his most famous books, including "The Adventures of Tom Sawyer" and "Huckleberry Finn."

The study was given to Elmira College in the 1950s and now resides on campus. Likewise, Quarry Farm now serves as a home for Twain scholars visiting the college. The study and a Twain exhibit center are open to visitors during the summer and contain original photographs, furniture and other memorabilia [www.elmira.edu/academics/ar_marktwain.shtml]. A statue of the author stands on the college campus, and the Clemens Center, a local performing arts facility, is named for him. Twain, his wife and children are buried in Elmira's Woodlawn Cemetery.

Elmira is hoping to promote Twain's legacy by bringing more tourists to the area, just as the other places he called home – Hannibal, Missouri and Hartford, Connecticut – have done. The local visitors bureau has considered starting a humor festival in Twain's name and would like to develop other attractions.

There are a number of independent bookstores in town that could only benefit from the effort.

AFTERWORD

Today more than ever, people need a sense of community. They want to belong – to go someplace where they feel at home. Independent bookstores are vital for that very reason. They're cultural centers. They provide sanctuary. They add character to the neighborhood and help to define the city.

To say booklovers are passionate about their favorite bookstores is an understatement. Going there isn't just something to do – an errand or a past-time. It's a way of life, a philosophy, a window on the world. Booklovers know that reading a book is a type of travel that takes them places, introduces them to other cultures, lets them explore, gives them experiences they may not have otherwise.

Indie booksellers stock titles that you're not likely to find anywhere else. They may not be on the bestseller list, but they may sit in a privileged spot on your bookshelf for the rest of your life. You can't put a pricetag on that kind of serendipity. Sure, the indies want to be commercially viable, but they wear their uniqueness – their funkiness, their oddities and eccentricities – like a badge of honor. They're not cookie-cutter clones of one another, they're about freedom of expression, giving readers more choices, offering a different perspective.

Indie booksellers are activists, too. When an issue or problem captures a community's attention, local bookstores get involved. Often, they're the starting place for word-of-mouth. They promote something that needs to be promoted, or they help to shoot down what needs to be shot down. They have a vested interest. They're committed. They'll stick out the bad times and won't pull up stakes at the first sign of an economic downturn.

It's bookselling without excuses. It's the enormity of Powell's in Portland, Oregon, and the college-town feel of Carytown Books in Richmond, Virginia. It's the independent streak of Book People in Austin, Texas, and the "Left Coast" charm of the former Midnight Special in Santa Monica. It's the nightly author readings at Politics & Prose in Washington, D.C., and the urban oasis of Three Lives & Company in New York City.

When one of them disappears, it's a loss for everybody.

This book is just the beginning of Bookstore Tourism. It only scratches the surface of what can be done with the concept. So, it's up to you to take the idea and run with it.

Anyone who has a little creativity and some basic organization skills can come up with endless variations on the basics I've covered. If you give it some thought and brainstorm with a friend or two (or 10 or 20), you'll find as I have that there are countless ways to create bookstore road trips – for yourselves, your organization, your local booksellers, or even your town.

As you launch Bookstore Tourism in your community, I hope you'll contact me and let me know what you and your group are doing. Future expanded editions of this book will feature interviews with you, details about your trips, your ideas and suggestions, your itineraries, your success stories, your cautionary tales, and most important, how Bookstore Tourism has benefited the independent bookshops in your favorite bookstore town. Maybe your town will do a bookstore exchange trip with another town. Maybe you'll create "Bookstore Sister Cities." If so, I'd like to hear about it.

Please write to me at the postal or e-mail address below. I'll do my best to respond personally to everyone who writes.

Also, because I'd like to create regional or city guides for bookstore road trips in the near future, I hope you'll pass along information about great bookshops or bookstore towns that you're familiar with. It can be the shop around the corner, or the one you just discovered halfway across the country.

I'm also interested in knowing about famous or even infamous bookstores, either currently in existence or long gone, particularly if they were a favorite hangout of well-known authors, playwrights or poets. I'm considering a large (coffee table) picture book on the topic, with the copy written by the authors themselves.

I'm also thinking ahead to "Bookstore Tourism International." Sound intriguing? Let me know!

The series of Bookstore Tourism books I'm proposing promises to bring well-deserved attention to independent booksellers everywhere, and to fill a publishing niche that I'm quite sure booklovers are craving.

Tell your friends about Bookstore Tourism. Get something started now!

Larry Portzline
Bookshop Junkie Press
P.O. Box 6067, Harrisburg, PA 17112
info@bookstoretourism.com
(Note: All material received becomes the property of Bookshop Junkie Press)

APPENDIX

National Booksellers Associations

American Booksellers Association
www.bookweb.org
(Book Sense program:
www.booksense.com)
(800) 637-0037

Association of Booksellers for Children
www.abfc.com
(800) 421-1665

Christian Booksellers Association
www.cbaonline.org
(800) 252-1950

National Association of College Stores
www.nacs.org
(800) 622-7498

Regional Booksellers Associations

Great Lakes Booksellers Association
Illinois, Indiana, Michigan and Ohio
www.books-glba.org
(800) 745-2460

Mid-South Independent Booksellers Association
Arkansas, Kansas, Louisiana, Mississippi, Missouri, Oklahoma, Tennessee, Texas
www.msiba.org
(877) 357-0757

Mountains & Plains Booksellers Association
Arizona, Colorado, Kansas, Nebraska, New Mexico, Utah, Wyoming
www.mountainsplains.org
(800) 752-0249

New Atlantic Independent Booksellers Association
Delaware, District of Columbia, Maryland, New Jersey, New York, Pennsylvania, Virginia
www.naiba.com
(877) 866-2422

New England Booksellers Association
Connecticut, Maine, Massachusetts, New Hampshire, New York, Rhode Island, Vermont
www.newenglandbooks.org
(800) 466-8711

Northern California Independent Booksellers Association
California, Nevada
www.nciba.com
(415) 561-7686

Pacific Northwest Booksellers Association
Alaska, Idaho, Montana, Oregon, Washington
www.pnba.org
(541) 683-4363

Southeast Booksellers Association
Alabama, Arkansas, Florida, Georgia, Kentucky, Louisiana, Mississippi, North Carolina, South Carolina, Tennessee, Virginia
www.sebaweb.org
(800) 331-9617

Southern California Booksellers Association
Arizona, California, Nevada
www.scbabooks.org
(626) 792-8435

Upper Midwest Booksellers Association
Illinois, Iowa, Kansas, Minnesota,
Missouri, Nebraska, North Dakota, South
Dakota, Wisconsin
www.abookaday.com
(800) 784-7522

U.S. Literary & Book Festivals

This is by no means a comprehensive list
of the many book fairs and literary festivals
that are held all around the country. For
more complete listings, or to search by
state, please visit the Library of Congress'
Center for the Book website at
http://lcweb.loc.gov/loc/cfbook/bookfair.h
tml. Please keep in mind that locations,
dates and contact information can change.

For book festivals near you, you can also
ask your local independent bookseller,
library, college, arts association or newspaper.

Alabama Bound Festival
Birmingham, AL
www.alabamabound.org
(205) 226-3610
April

Ann Arbor Book Festival
Ann Arbor, MI
www.aabookfestival.org
(734) 662-7407
May

Arizona Book Festival
Phoenix, AZ
www.azbookfestival.org/index.html
(602) 257-0335
April

Atlanta Book Festival
Atlanta, GA
www.atlantabookfestival.com
(404) 259-4841
September

Baltimore Book Festival
Baltimore, MD
www.bop.org/calendar/events/book_ind
ex.html
(410) 752-8632
September

BookExpo America
Location changes
www.bookexpo.reedexpo.com
(800) 840-5614
May-June

Border Book Festival
Mesilla, NM
www.borderbookfestival.org
(505) 524-1499
April

Boston Globe Book Festival
Boston, MA
www.bostonglobe.com/community/pro-
grams/books.stm
(617) 929-2641
October

**Boston International Antiquarian
Book Fair**
Boston, MA
www.bostonbookfair.com
e-mail: info@bostonbookfair.com
November

Buckeye Book Fair
Wooster, OH
www.buckeyebookfair.com
(330) 262-3244
November

**Bumbershoot, the Seattle
Arts Festival**
Seattle, WA
www.bumbershoot.org
(206) 281-7788
September

**California International Antiquarian
Book Fair**
San Francisco, CA
www.sfbookfair.com
(800) 454-6041
February

Delaware Authors Day
Dover, DE
www.state.de.us/heritage/authors.htm
(302) 577-5044
November

Fall for the Book Festival
Fairfax, VA
www.fallforthebook.org
(202) 334-4740
September

Georgia Literary Festival
Location changes
www.gsu.edu/~wwwgte/
August

Great Salt Lake Book Festival
Salt Lake City, UT
www.utahhumanities.org/bookfestival/bookfestival2004.php
(801) 359-9670
September

Harlem Book Fair
New York, NY
www.qbr.com/hbf
(212) 348-1681
July

High Plains BookFest
Billings, MT
www.downtownbillings.com
(406) 248-1685
July

Kentucky Book Fair
Frankfort, KY
www.kybookfair.com
(502) 564-8300, ext. 297
November

Los Angeles Times Festival of Books
Los Angeles, CA
www.latimes.com/extras/festivalofbooks
(800) LATIMES, ext. 7BOOK
April

Louisiana Book Festival
Baton Rouge, LA
http://lbf.state.lib.la.us
(888) 487-2700
November

Miami Book Fair International
Miami, FL
www.miamibookfair.com
(305) 237-3258
November

Montana Festival Of The Book
Missoula, MT
www.bookfest-mt.org
(406) 243-6022
October

National Book Festival
Washington, DC
www.loc.gov/bookfest
(888) 714-4696
October

National Press Club Book Fair
Washington, DC
http://npc.press.org
(202) 662-7564
November

Nebraska Book Festival
Kearney, NE
www.unk.edu/acad/english/nebraska-bookfestival/home.html
September

New Orleans Book Fair
New Orleans, LA
www.nolabookfair.com
October

New York Antiquarian Book Fair
New York, NY
www.sanfordsmith.com/nyabookfair
(212) 777.5218
April-May

New York Is Book Country
New York, NY
www.nyisbookcountry.com
(646) 557-6400
September

North Carolina Literary Festival
Chapel Hill, NC
www.lib.unc.edu/nclitfest
April

Northern Arizona Book Festival
Flagstaff, AZ
www.flagstaffcentral.com/bookfest
(928) 774-9118
April

Ohio River Festival of Books
Huntington, WV
www.ohioriverbooks.org
(304) 528-5700
May

Printers Row Book Fair
Chicago, IL
www.printersrowbookfair.org
(312) 987-9896
June

St. Petersburg Times Festival of Reading
St. Petersburg, FL
www.festivalofreading.com
(727) 445-4142
November

Santa Fe Festival of the Book
Santa Fe, NM
www.santafelibrary.org/festival.html
(505) 955-4866
October

Sarasota Reading Festival
Sarasota, FL
www.sarasotareadingfestival.com
(941) 308-7323
November

Seattle Antiquarian Book Fair
Seattle, WA
www.seattlebookfair.com
(206) 323-3999
October

Small Press Book Fair
New York, NY
www.smallpress.org/bookfair/bookfair.htm
(212) 764-7021
March

South Carolina Book Festival
Columbia, SC
www.schumanities.org/bookfestival.htm
(803) 691-4100
February

Southern Festival of Books
Nashville, TN
www.tn-humanities.org/sfbmain.htm
(615) 320-7001
October

Southern Kentucky Festival of Books
Bowling Green, KY
www.sokybookfest.org
(270) 745-5016
April

Tennessee Williams/New Orleans Literary Festival
New Orleans, LA
www.tennesseewilliams.net
(504) 581-1144
March-April

Texas Book Festival
Austin, TX
www.texasbookfestival.org
(512) 477-4055
October

Twin Cities Book Festival
Minneapolis, MN
www.raintaxi.com/bookfest
(612) 825-1528
October

Vegas Valley Book Festival
Henderson and Las Vegas, NV
www.vegasvalleybookfest.org
e-mail: info@vegasvalleybookfest.org
October

Virginia Festival of the Book
Charlottesville, VA
www.vabook.org
(434) 924-6890
March

West Virginia Book Festival
Charleston, WV
www.wvhumanities.org/bookfest/book-fest.htm
(304) 343-4646
October

Some Wonderful Books About Books, Bookstores, and Reading Groups

- "Among the Gently Mad: Strategies and Perspectives for the Book Hunter in the 21st Century" – Nicholas A. Basbanes

- "Book Collecting: A Comprehensive Guide" – Allen and Patricia Ahearn

- "The Book Group Book: A Thoughtful Guide to Forming and Enjoying a Stimulating Book Discussion Group" – Ellen Slezak

- "Book Lust: Recommended Reading for Every Mood, Moment, and Reason" – Nancy Pearl

- "Book Row: An Anecdotal and Pictorial History of the Antiquarian Book Trade" – Marvin Mondlin and Roy Meador

- "The Book That Changed My Life: Interviews With National Book Award Winners and Finalists" – Diane Osen

- "The Booklover's Repair Kit: First Aid for Home Libraries" – Estelle Ellis, Wilton Wiggins and Douglas Lee

- "Books That Changed the World" – Robert B. Downs

- "Ex Libris: Confessions of a Common Reader" – Anne Fadiman

- "A Gentle Madness: Bibliophiles, Bibliomanes, and the Eternal Passion for Books" – Nicholas A. Basbanes

- "In the Stacks: Short Stories About Libraries & Librarians" – Michael Cart

- "The Literature Lover's Book of Lists" – Judie L.H. Strouf

- "The New York Public Library Guide to Reading Groups" – Rollene Saal

- "A Pound of Paper: Confessions of a Book Addict" – John Baxter

- "The Readers' Choice: 200 Book Club Favorites" – Victoria Golden McMains
- "The Reading Group Book: The Complete Guide to Starting and Sustaining a Reading Group, With Annotated Lists of 250 Titles for Provocative Discussion" – David Laskin and Holly Hughes
- "The Reading Group Handbook: Everything You Need to Know to Start Your Own Book Club" – Rachel W. Jacobsohn
- "The Reading List Contemporary Fiction: A Critical Guide to the Complete Works of 110 Authors" – David Rubel
- "Required Reading" – Andred DelBanco
- "Shelf Life: Romance, Mystery, Drama, and Other Page-Turning Adventures from a Year in a Bookstore" – Suzanne Strempek Shea
- "Sixpence House: Lost in a Town of Books" – Paul Collins
- "So Many Books, So Little Time: A Year of Passionate Reading" – Sara Nelson
- "What to Read: The Essential Guide for Reading Group Members and Other Booklovers" – Mickey Pearlman
- "A Year of Reading: A Month-By-Month Guide to Classics and Crowd-Pleasers for You and Your Book Group" – Elisabeth Ellington and Jane Freimiller

State Resources

The following is a comprehensive list of state agencies and bureaus dealing with the arts, economic development, history, libraries and tourism. Their websites are included so you can find more information and contact the agency to determine how they might be able to assist you with your Bookstore Tourism efforts.

Many of these websites offer news and updates about their services and programs, suggestions for things to do and places to visit, educational resources, regional and local information, maps, event calendars, publications, guidebooks, directories, workshop schedules, demographics, product information, legislative updates and links to other useful resources.

Each agency's Web address was current at the time of publication:

Alabama
Arts: www.arts.state.al.us
Econ. Dev.: www.ado.state.al.us
Historical: www.archives.state.al.us
Library Assoc.: http://allanet.org
Tourism: www.touralabama.org

Alaska
Arts: www.educ.state.ak.us/aksca
Econ. Dev.: www.dced.state.ak.us
Historical:
www.alaskahistoricalsociety.org
Library Assoc.: www.akla.org
Tourism: www.travelalaska.com

Arizona
Arts: www.arizonaarts.org
Econ. Dev.: www.azcommerce.com
Historical: w3.arizona.edu/ ~ azhist
Library Assoc.: http://azla.org
Tourism: www.arizonaguide.com

Arkansas
Arts: www.arkansasarts.com
Econ. Dev.:
www.1800arkansas.com/home.cfm
Historical:
http://www.uark.edu/depts/arkhist/home
Library Assoc.: www.arlib.org
Tourism: www.arkansas.com

California
Arts: www.cac.ca.gov
Econ. Dev.:
www.commerce.ca.gov/state/ttca/ttca_h
omepage.jsp
Historical: www.calhist.org
Library Assoc.: www.cla-net.org
Tourism: www.visitcalifornia.com

Colorado
Arts: www.coloarts.state.co.us
Econ. Dev.:
www.state.co.us/gov_dir/oed.html
Historical:
www.gtownloop.com/chs.html
Library Assoc.: www.cla-web.org
Tourism: www.colorado.com

Connecticut
Arts: www.ctarts.org
Econ. Dev.:
www.ct.gov/ecd/site/default.asp
Historical: www.chs.org
Library Assoc.: http://cla.uconn.edu
Tourism: www.tourism.state.ct.us

Delaware
Arts: www.artsdel.org
Econ. Dev.:
www.state.de.us/dedo/index.htm
Historical: www.hsd.org
Library Assoc.:
www.dla.lib.de.us/index.shtml
Tourism: www.visitdelaware.net

Florida
Arts: www.dos.state.fl.us
Econ. Dev.: www.myflorida.com/myflori-
da/government/governorinitiatives/otted
Historical: www.florida-historical-soc.org
Library Assoc.: www.flalib.org
Tourism: www.flausa.com

Georgia
Arts: www.ganet.org/georgia-arts
Econ. Dev.:
www.georgia.org/economic/index.asp
Historical: www.georgiahistory.com
Library Assoc.: wwwlib.gsu.edu/gla
Tourism: www.georgia.org

Hawaii
Arts: www.state.hi.us/sfca
Econ. Dev.: www.hawaii.gov/dbedt
Historical: www.hawaiianhistory.org
Library Assoc.: www2.hawaii.edu/hla
Tourism: www.gohawaii.com

Idaho
Arts: www.state.id.us/arts
Econ. Dev.: www.idoc.state.id.us
Historical: www.idahohistory.net
Library Assoc.: www.idaholibraries.org
Tourism: www.visitid.org

Illinois
Arts: www.state.il.us/agency/iac
Econ. Dev.: www.commerce.state.il.us
Historical: www.historyillinois.org
Library Assoc.: www.ila.org
Tourism: www.enjoyillinois.com

Indiana
Arts: www.state.in.us/iac
Econ. Dev.: www.ai.org/doc/index.html
Historical: www.indianahistory.org
Library Assoc.: www.ilfonline.org
Tourism: www.in.gov/enjoyindiana

Iowa
Arts: www.culturalaffairs.org
Econ. Dev.: www.state.ia.us/ided
Historical: www.iowahistory.org
Library Assoc.: www.iren.net/acrl
Tourism: www.traveliowa.com

Kansas
Arts: arts.state.ks.us
Econ. Dev.: www.kansascommerce.com
Historical: www.kshs.org
Library Assoc.:
http://skyways.lib.ks.us/kansas/kla
Tourism: www.accesskansas.org

Kentucky
Arts: www.kyarts.org
Econ. Dev.: www.thinkkentucky.com
Historical: http://history.ky.gov
Library Assoc.: www.kylibasn.org
Tourism: www.kytourism.com

Louisiana
Arts: www.crt.state.la.us/arts/index.htm
Econ. Dev.: www.lded.state.la.us
Historical: www.louisianahistoricalsociety.org
Library Assoc.: www.llaonline.org
Tourism: www.crt.state.la.us

Maine
Arts: www.mainearts.com
Econ. Dev.: www.econdevmaine.com
Historical: www.mainehistory.com
Library Assoc.: http://mainelibraries.org
Tourism: www.visitmaine.com

Maryland
Arts: www.msac.org
Econ. Dev.: www.dbed.state.md.us
Historical: www.mdhs.org
Library Assoc.: www.mdlib.org
Tourism: www.mdisfun.org

Massachusetts
Arts: www.massculturalcouncil.org
Econ. Dev.:
www.state.ma.us/econ/index.htm
Historical:
www.magnet.state.ma.us/sec/mhc
Library Assoc.: www.masslib.org
Tourism: www.mass-vacation.com

Michigan
Arts: www.michigan.gov/hal
Econ. Dev.:
www.medc.michigan.org/index_flash.asp
?homepage = index.asp
Historical: www.h-net.msu.edu/ ~ hsm
Library Assoc.: www.mla.lib.mi.us
Tourism: www.travel.michigan.org

Minnesota
Arts: www.arts.state.mn.us
Econ. Dev.: www.commerce.state.mn.us
Historical: www.mnhs.org
Library Assoc.:
http://mnlibraryAssoc..org
Tourism: www2.exploreminnesota.com

Mississippi
Arts: www.arts.state.ms.us
Econ. Dev.: www.mississippi.org
Historical:
www.mdah.state.ms.us/admin/mhistsoc.html
Library Assoc.: www.misslib.org
Tourism: www.visitmississippi.org

Missouri
Arts: www.missouriartscouncil.org
Econ. Dev.: www.ded.state.mo.us
Historical: www.system.missouri.edu/shs
Library Assoc.: www.molib.org
Tourism: www.missouritourism.org

Montana
Arts: www.art.state.mt.us
Econ. Dev.: www.commerce.state.mt.us
Historical: www.his.state.mt.us
Library Assoc.: www.mtlib.org
Tourism: www.visitmt.com

Nebraska
Arts: www.nebraskaartscouncil.org
Econ. Dev.: www.neded.org
Historical: www.nebraskahistory.org
Library Assoc.: www.nol.org/home/NLA
Tourism: www.visitnebraska.org

Nevada
Arts: dmla.clan.lib.nv.us/docs/arts
Econ. Dev.: www.expand2nevada.com
Historical:
http://dmla.clan.lib.nv.us/docs/museums/reno/his-soc.htm
Library Assoc.: www.nevadalibraries.org
Tourism: www.travelnevada.com

New Hampshire
Arts: www.state.nh.us/nharts
Econ. Dev.:
www.nheconomy.com/nheconomy/dredweb/main/index.php
Historical: www.nhhistory.org
Library Assoc.: www.state.nh.us/nhla
Tourism: www.visitnh.gov

New Jersey
Arts: www.njartscouncil.org
Econ. Dev.:
www.state.nj.us/commerce/index.htm
Historical: www.jerseyhistory.org
Library Assoc.: www.njla.org
Tourism: www.state.nj.us

New Mexico
Arts: www.nmarts.org
Econ. Dev.: www.edd.state.nm.us
Historical: www.hsnm.org
Library Assoc.: www.nmla.org
Tourism: www.newmexico.org

New York
Arts: www.nysca.org
Econ. Dev.:
www.nylovesbiz.com/default.asp
Historical: www.nyhistory.org
New York
Library Assoc.: www.nyla.org
Tourism: www.iloveny.state.ny.us

North Carolina
Arts: www.ncarts.org
Econ. Dev.: www.commerce.state.nc.us
Historical: www.ah.dcr.state.nc.us
Library Assoc.: www.nclaonline.org
Tourism: www.visit.nc.org

North Dakota
Arts: www.state.nd.us/arts
Econ. Dev.: www.growingnd.com
Historical: www.state.nd.us/hist/org.htm
Library Assoc.:
http://ndsl.lib.state.nd.us/ndla
Tourism: www.discovernd.com

Ohio
Arts: www.oac.state.oh.us
Econ. Dev.: www.odod.state.oh.us
Historical: www.ohiohistory.org
Library Assoc.: www.olc.org
Tourism: www.ohiotourism.com

Oklahoma
Arts: www.oklaosf.state.ok.us/ ~ arts
Econ. Dev.: www.odoc.state.ok.us
Historical: www.ok-history.mus.ok.us
Library Assoc.: www.oklibs.org
Tourism: www.travelok.com

Oregon
Arts:
www.oregonartscommission.org/main.php
Econ. Dev.: www.econ.state.or.us
Historical: www.ohs.org
Library Assoc.: www.olaweb.org
Tourism: www.traveloregon.com

Pennsylvania
Arts: www.artsnet.org/pca
Econ. Dev.: www.inventpa.com
Historical: www.hsp.org
Library Assoc.: www.palibraries.org
Tourism: www.experiencepa.com

Rhode Island
Arts: www.risca.state.ri.us
Econ. Dev.: www.riedc.com
Historical: www.rihs.org
Library Assoc.:
www.uri.edu/library/rila/rila.html
Tourism: www.VisitRhodeIsland.com

South Carolina
Arts: www.state.sc.us/arts
Econ. Dev.: www.callsouthcarolina.com
Historical: www.schistory.org
Library Assoc.: www.scla.org
Tourism:
www.discoversouthcarolina.com

South Dakota
Arts:
www.state.sd.us/deca/sdarts/index.htm
Econ. Dev.: www.state.sd.us/goed
Historical: www.sdhistory.org
Library Assoc.: www.usd.edu/sdla
Tourism: www.travelsd.com

Tennessee
Arts: www.arts.state.tn.us
Econ. Dev.: www.state.tn.us/ecd
Historical: www.tennesseehistory.com
Library Assoc.: www.lib.utk.edu/~tla
Tourism: www.tnvacation.com

Texas
Arts: www.arts.state.tx.us
Econ. Dev.: www.txed.state.tx.us
Historical: www.tsha.utexas.edu
Library Assoc.: www.txla.org
Tourism: www.traveltex.com

Utah
Arts: www.arts.utah.org
Econ. Dev.: www.dced.utah.gov/business/business.html
Historical: http://history.utah.gov
Library Assoc.: www.ula.org
Tourism: www.utah.com

Vermont
Arts: www.vermontartscouncil.org
Econ. Dev.: www.ThinkVermont.com
Historical: www.vermonthistory.org
Library Assoc.:
www.vermontlibraries.org
Tourism: www.1-800-vermont.com

Virginia
Arts: www.arts.state.va.us
Econ. Dev.: www.yesvirginia.org
Historical: www.vahistorical.org
Library Assoc.: www.vla.org
Tourism: www.virginia.org

Washington
Arts: www.arts.wa.gov
Econ. Dev.: www.cted.wa.gov
Historical:
www.washingtonhistory.org/wshs
Library Assoc.: www.wla.org
Tourism: www.tourism.wa.gov

West Virginia
Arts: www.wvculture.org
Econ. Dev.: www.wvdo.org
Historical: www.wvhistorical.com
Library Assoc.: www.wvla.org
Tourism: www.callwva.com

Wisconsin
Arts: www.arts.state.wi.us
Econ. Dev.: www.wheda.com
Historical: www.wisconsinhistory.org
Library Assoc.: www.wla.lib.wi.us
Tourism: www.tourism.state.wi.us

Wyoming
Arts: wyoarts.state.wy.us
Econ. Dev.: www.wyomingbusiness.org
Historical: http://wyshs.org
Library Assoc.: www.wyla.org
Tourism: www.wyomingtourism.org

DATE DUE

JUN 17 2006			
MAY 12 2007			

Printed in the United States
38347LV

GAYLORD   PRINTED IN U.S.A.

0975 893401